848.91707 B43j
Benabou, Marcel.
Jacob, Menahem, and Mimoun

Jacob, Menahem, and Mimoun

STAGES · VOLUME 11 · SERIES EDITORS
Michael Holquist, *Yale University*
Warren Motte, *University of Colorado at Boulder*
Gerald Prince, *University of Pennsylvania*
Patricia Meyer Spacks, *University of Virginia*

MARCEL BÉNABOU

Jacob, Menahem, and Mimoun

Jacob, Ménahem et Mimoun: Une Épopée familiale

A Family Epic

Translated by Steven Rendall

UNIVERSITY OF NEBRASKA PRESS

LINCOLN AND LONDON

Originally published in French as *Jacob, Ménahem, et Mimoun: Une Épopée familiale,* © Editions du Seuil, La Librairie du xxᵉ siècle, collection dirigée par Maurice Olender. Preface and translation © 1998 by the University of Nebraska Press All rights reserved. Manufactured in the United States of America. ⊛ The paper in this book meets the minimum requirements of American National Standard for Information Sciences – Permanence of Paper for Printed Library Materials, ANSI Z39.48-1984.

Library of Congress Cataloging-in-Publication Data
Bénabou, Marcel.
[Jacob, Menahem et Mimoun. English] Jacob, Menahem, and Mimoun: a famly epic / Marcel Bénabou;
Translated by Steven Rendall. p. cm. – (Stages; v. 11)
Includes bibliographical references and index.
ISBN 0-8032-1285-2 (cl) I. Rendall, Steven. II. Title.
III. Series: Stages (Series); v. 11.
PQ2662.E4714J3313 1998 848'.91407 – dc21
97-27988 CIP

CONTENTS

One Always Writes the Same Preface vii

Incipit 3

Vocation 7

Book 39

Resources 67

Models 95

Uncertain Ancestors 119

The Two Orphans 143

Intermittencies 177

The Turning Point 199

Over and Over 217

One Always Writes the Same Preface
WARREN MOTTE

The title that Marcel Bénabou originally chose for this volume was 'One Always Writes the Same Book.' And from every perspective – with the crucial exception of his French publishers – it was a very wonderful title indeed. Like the titles of his two previous books, *Pourquoi je n'ai écrit aucun de mes livres* (1986; *Why I Have Not Written Any of My Books*, 1996) and *Jette ce livre avant qu'il soit trop tard* (1992; Throw this book away before it's too late), it was both an apt characterization of the work it designated and gleefully duplicitous. *Why I Have Not Written Any of My Books* is a lamentation on the impossibility of writing and a general (if deeply insincere) apology for the fact that Bénabou, born to writing, had failed to produce any books. Yet the book itself belies its title, obviously enough – as does the fact that, despite his claim, Bénabou had published an earlier book, a scholarly volume entitled *La Résistance africaine à la romanisation* (1976; The African resistance to romanization). *Jette ce livre avant qu'il soit trop tard* warns its reader, with high irony, of the dangers of literature: how fiction can contaminate one's life, what happens when one begins to live through books – living, precisely, in order to have something to write *about*. But of course the injunction that title enunciates is the very last thing Bénabou wants his reader to do. And in any case, in French literature of the latter part of the twentieth century, it's *always* too late.

By the same token, 'One Always Writes the Same Book' may be seen both as an apposite description of the work it was intended to designate, and as an outright – but genial – lie. On the one hand, Bénabou is truly persuaded that a writer's work is necessarily iterative, that a writer's books cohere mutually in a sort of palimpsest arrangement, 'for I am convinced,' he tells us in the final paragraph of *this* book, 'that one always writes the same book.' (I should confess here that, having written the preface for *Why I Have Not Written Any of My Books*, I am in *this* preface preternaturally chary of the notion of redundancy, and consequently I shall deal with it exclusively as a theoretical issue rather than a practical one.) On the other hand, for anyone familiar with Bénabou's writings it becomes apparent in the first few pages that this book is not quite like the others. On the third hand (I'm referring to that freakish appendage of the literary imagination that an author uses to hold a pen, and a reader to turn the pages, one after another), Bénabou's original title suggests enticingly that fearful symmetries prevail among his works. For all three titles contain the word *book* and lead us to suspect that the notion of the book itself is Bénabou's central concern. There's a neat distribution of voice in those titles, too, from first person to second person to third person: is Bénabou trying to persuade his benighted reader that his books are going somewhere? Moreover, those titles outline an issue that Bénabou wishes us to consider with wild surmise: together, his books strain toward something far vaster than any single book, something that might approximate the impossible dimensions of, well, *epic*.

But it was not to be, alas: Marcel Bénabou's publishers refused 'One Always Writes the Same Book,' and they settled instead on *Jacob, Ménahem et Mimoun: Une Épopée familiale*, a title that is in many ways just as wily and vexed as the original, if perhaps more subtly. For despite what its title so blithely adumbrates, this book, like Bénabou's others, is impossible to categorize generically. At times it reads like an autobiography, at others like a novel; sometimes it resembles historiography, sometimes an essay on literary theory. Bénabou does evoke the epic genre in his title, but this is a book that is intended to interrogate, rather than illustrate, that literary form. His questioning is constant and subversive, subterranean as it were; its vehicles are deliberate understatement and the cruelest sort of irony. To his credit, Bénabou frets about the issue of genre, wondering aloud on the page how the various and disparate directions he feels compelled to pursue can be made to cohere in what he can only term, provisionally, an 'oeuvre.' It's not the only thing he worries about: in point of fact *Jacob, Menahem, and Mimoun: A Family Epic* sketches out an exhaustive catalogue of every kind of doubt that can assail a writer in our time.

Most of all, Bénabou worries about what he calls his 'debts.' Initially at least, he identifies two debts. First, having been born in 1939 into a Jewish family in Meknès, Morocco, Bénabou survived the Holocaust unscathed. Through no fault of his own, he carefully points out, but merely by accident. He owes his second debt to his parents. As the seventh of eight children, and the last male child in the family, Bénabou sensed early on that his parents would have wished him to become a rabbi. But that was not to be, either: at the age of seventeen, Bénabou left Morocco and went to Paris, where he enrolled in the Lycée Louis-le-Grand and gained admission to the prestigious École Normale Supérieure. He took his doctorate at the Sorbonne and became a professor of Roman history at the University of Paris, where he remains to this day. In short, he did become a teacher – but a resolutely secularist one. Other debts soon become apparent. He feels that he owes something to the broader Jewish community in Morocco. All the more so since that Sephardic community was marginalized with regard to the Ashkenazic European tradition and progressively decimated through emigration to Israel, France, and Canada. Some account of it must be given, he senses, before it disappears entirely. Bénabou worries too about his distance from his family and that community. His literal distance, to be sure, but also – and perhaps primarily – his figural distance. He had sailed away, he suggests, on the wine-dark sea of literature, secular literature. Finally, in one of those perverse twists that conscience plays even on the best of us, Bénabou feels deeply indebted to the very literary tradition through which he absconded, to the books that shaped him as an intellectual.

Bénabou wonders if, through writing his past, he may begin to liquidate those debts. For the burning issue in this book is the past – or, more precisely, the way Bénabou *remembers* the past. He experiences his memory like an illness; yet he wonders if, through writing, he might turn the affliction into the cure. The initiatory gesture of *Jacob, Menahem, and Mimoun: A Family Epic* is a mnemonic one: the first sentence of the book is itself a memory, Bénabou tells us. He had drafted it more than thirty years ago, in the library of the École Normale Supérieure, intending it as the incipit of his first book. It was a luminous sentence, and full of portent; yet everything he tried to write after it seemed pale and inadequate in comparison. That anecdote is a lovely fable of writing. And a harrowing one for anyone who takes writing seriously. Especially for Bénabou himself, because nobody – not Flaubert, not Proust, not even Kafka in his most obsessive moments – takes writing quite as seriously as he does. Or so he feels, at least.

If that is Marcel Bénabou's distinction as a writer (or rather a would-be writer), it is also his most crippling handicap. He lives and breathes literature from within, but he can't get outside it long enough to write it. He is forced to realize that, in his case, even those things that he imagined would enable him to write serve, on the contrary, to paralyze him. Thus for instance memory, and the desire to save something, whether it be the daily life of the Jewish community in Meknès or a sentence written thirty years ago, from oblivion. He discovers that his memory of things past is hypertrophic: the problem is not that he can't remember, but that he remembers all too much. When Bénabou compares the content of his memory to the content of his writing, the richness of the one mocks the poverty of the other, and he despairs.

But not for long – at least in terms of geological time. For he has his vocation to consider, and he has always known that one day, by hook or by crook, he would become a writer. His desire is modest enough: he wishes merely to recapture the privileged status he enjoyed within his family circle as a child, 'to become again, as I had once been, not a person who speaks about others, but one about whom others speak.' Yet families are one thing, and literary traditions are quite another; and the dimensions of the latter beggar those of the former. Moreover, who will speak about Bénabou in the literary community if he doesn't speak *about* himself first? The writing of the self thus seems to him a logical and necessary place to start. He gazes unflinchingly into the mirror of the past in this book, speculating on the image of himself which he finds there. He quotes a passage from Apuleius where the author praises mirrors and argues that nothing is more worthy of a person's consideration than his or her own reflected image. But Bénabou is not a classicist for nothing, and the cautionary tale of Narcissus troubles him, too. Toward the end of *Jacob, Menahem, and Mimoun* he wonders if, despite all his vigilance, he has not fallen into the pool of the ego: wishing to write about his people, he finds that he has written almost exclusively about himself.

If the ego is a problem for Bénabou, the issue of the 'other' is no less thorny. Especially when it comes to writing, because in order to write, Bénabou must seek to learn how others have written. In fact, much of *Jacob, Menahem, and Mimoun* can be read as the account of one man's quest for a literary model.

Bénabou speaks of the 'intellectual gymnastics' he engages in when he encounters new narrative forms and tries to appropriate them and alludes ironically to his 'nascent mimetic bulimia.' Examples of 'solidly constructed books' pique his imagination the most, books with an elaborate and savant structural armature. Yet his search for narrative models founders on the same rocks as his quest for memory: it is not that he fails to identify a performative model, but rather that models occur to him in devastating, bewildering superabundance. His only recourse is to deploy that very superabundance in the pages of his own book. Throughout *Jacob, Menahem, and Mimoun* Bénabou refers to his experience of Jewish sacred writings, principally the Torah, Gemara, and Mishnah. Those allusions are buried, however, under an avalanche of references to other literary traditions, as Bénabou paints in broad strokes the panorama of his literary horizon. He refers to Homer and Virgil, those masters of the classical epic form, five times each. He alludes as well, simply in passing or in more detail, to a staggering variety of other literary figures (I intend the following catalog as a gestalt whose integers signify most pungently in a collective manner, rather than particularly – for that is how they function in this book – and I beg the reader to buckle his or her seatbelt and *hang on*): Euripides, Epicurus, Cicero, Livy, Tacitus, Tertullian, Apuleius, Plotinus, St. Augustine, Dante, Annius of Viterbo, Ronsard, Montaigne, Shakespeare, Descartes, Corneille, La Fontaine, Spinoza, Racine, Voltaire, Rousseau, Diderot, Sade, Louis-Sébastien Mercier, Goethe, Joseph Joubert, Schelling, Schopenhauer, Alfred de Vigny, Heinrich Heine, Delacroix (the painter's *Journal*), Balzac, Hugo, Dumas *père,* Thackeray, Melville, Baudelaire, Flaubert, the Goncourt brothers, Jules Verne, Edmond About, Zola, Thomas Hardy, Odilon Redon (his *Journal*), Mallarmé, Pierre Loti, Isaac Leib Peretz, Joseph Conrad, Sholem Aleichem,

Israel Zangwill, Rudyard Kipling, H. G. Wells, Proust, Alfred Jarry, Thomas Mann, Rilke, Raymond Roussel, Amédée Achard, Jean Jalabert, Max du Veuzit, the Tharaud brothers, Edmond Fleg, Joyce, Kafka, György Lukács, Pierre Benoit, Franz Werfel, Jean Cocteau, Georges Bataille, Michel Leiris, Raymond Radiguet, Raymond Queneau, Sartre, Paul Nizan, Jean Genet, Lawrence Durrell, Maxence Van der Mersche, Camus, Roland Barthes, Louis Althusser, and Pierre Bourdieu.

Among all the literary allusions in *Jacob, Menahem, and Mimoun,* two are very largely occulted; yet they are crucially important to Bénabou and constitute determining influences in his development as a writer. When he suggests near the end of his book that he has 'succeeded only in getting lost in the labyrinth that I myself had meticulously built,' he is referring to the Oulipo, short for Ouvroir de Littérature Potentielle (Workshop of Potential Literature), a group of literary experimentalists that he joined in 1969 and which has colored his literary imagination ever since. Founded in 1960 by Raymond Queneau and François Le Lionnais and collectively devoted to the theory and practice of literary form, the Oulipo would come to include writers such as Italo Calvino, Jacques Roubaud, and Harry Mathews. Early in its existence, the members of the Oulipo adopted a definition of the group that resonates with characteristic irony and good cheer: 'Oilipians: rats who must build the labyrinth from which they propose to escape.' For the Oulipo is deeply interested in the notion of formal constraint and how it can structure writing. Viewed in broad perspective, the problem of constraint in its various manifestations – familial and social constraint, aesthetic constraint, personal constraint, and so forth – may be seen to animate much of *Jacob, Menahem, and Mimoun.*

The second oblique reference in this book is to Bénabou's friend Georges Perec, a fellow member of the Oulipo and the author of what is perhaps the richest body of work in contemporary French literature. Yet Bénabou never actually names Perec. When he speaks about collaborating on literary projects in the 1960s with 'a friend who died too soon,' he is referring to Perec (who died in 1982 at the age of 45). When he reflects later in the book upon his struggles to come to terms with his childhood, he says, 'And I came almost to envy a friend who, when I told him about my memory's unfurling, tartly replied in a challenging tone: "I have no childhood memories!"' It's the same friend, of course, and that challenging assertion is in fact the inaugural moment of Perec's own project of remembrance, *W ou le souvenir d'enfance* (1975; *W or The Memory of Childhood*, 1988), a book that figures more prominently than any other as a model for this one. When, finally, Bénabou worries about projecting too much of himself into the description of his ancestors, and the risk that 'they would ultimately seem to proceed from me, rather than I from them,' he is alluding to Vigny's celebrated phrase: 'If I write their history, they will be my descendants.' But it is also that phrase which Perec had chosen as the epigraph for a 'family novel' that he intended to write one day. Moreover, it is a phrase that enunciates, epigrammatically and with fine understatement, the cruel – and unequal – competition of the 'I' and the 'we' that dominates Bénabou's efforts to represent his 'family epic' within the covers of a book.

For that is the heart of the matter here: the book itself in all of its avatars, from its material, objective, dog-eared manifestations to its Platonic ideal. Bénabou senses that everything in his life, from his earliest years onward, has conspired, in effect, to make him write a book. But not just any book, alas. On that issue at least, the sacred and the secular traditions concur, and both weigh heavily upon Bénabou's shoulders. He was raised among the 'People of the Book,' as he puts it; and on his own initiative he became an adept of 'Mallarmean orthodoxy,' for whom beyond and above any given book The Book necessarily hovers, in its glorious – and inaccessible – virtuality. A deep respect for books was instilled in him very early on, as well as the idea that carelessness with books can result in 'the most terrible consequences.' Reading and praying have always been linked in his mind, Bénabou remarks. The word *book* is massively overdetermined in his lexicon; and whenever he utters it in *this* book, he is, in a very real sense, praying. For how can he pretend to write a book, if not through a process of intense devotion to the book itself? All the more so since he has always enshrined the book as an unattainable ideal, whether it be the case of the Judaic or Mallarmean Book, or indeed a more profane, more material – but no less capital – work such as *Madame Bovary* or *Remembrance of Things Past*. Bénabou determines stoically that his own project must fall into the hallowed category of 'impossible books,' because nothing short of that will do. Clearly enough, an axiom like that one will not immediately unlock the floodgates of literary creativity, and Bénabou voices the familiar lament of the impossibility of writing throughout *Jacob, Menahem, and Mimoun*, to great ironic effect. He plays frequently in the French original on the words *aboutir* (to result in, to achieve), *aboutissement* (outcome), and *inabouti* (unfinished, failed), impaling those homonyms of 'Bénabou' painfully and precisely on the horns of his writerly dilemma.

He would have us believe, in short, that his project is doomed in advance. And on the face of it, that notion is pretty convincing. For one thing, he has been trying to write this book for more than thirty years, he tells us. For another, the reach of his intent seems far too vast. He proposes to tell the history of the Jews of Morocco, doing for that community what others have done for the shtetls of Eastern Europe. He will accede to that general history through the particular story of his family, more particularly still through the stories of Jacob, his mother's grandfather, and Menahem and Mimoun, his own grandfathers. But merely shaking the family tree will not be enough, Bénabou argues. He dreams of a 'family novel.' But not a garden variety one; rather, 'one of those novelistic summas into which we enter as if for a long sojourn in a distant land.' A work that would 'let a little fresh air into French literature, which seemed to me, for the past few years, to have smelled a bit musty.' Nothing short of the epic will suit his purposes. At some level, despite the daunting dimensions that he projects for his book, we sympathize with Bénabou readily enough. For to a greater or lesser degree we all wish to live like heroes in an epic; we all experience 'the imperishable need' (as Johan Huizinga puts it) 'to live in beauty'; and we are constantly telling ourselves – and telling others around us, Lord love 'em – stories about ourselves in order to satisfy our need.

If anyone understands that need, it is Marcel Bénabou, and he will turn it to his advantage, playing on his reader's desire in *Jacob, Menahem, and Mimoun* even as he plays on his own. He invites us to look over his shoulder as he grapples with his problems. He asks us to consider along with him the various technical questions that he must adjudicate. How can objective documentation and subjective data be made to cohere in the architecture of his project? How can time be staged effectively here, and how can one move the story from one temporal frame to another and back again? How can he reconcile the three apparently dissimilar quests that animate his project, that is, the quest for history, for personal memory, and for literary form? Bénabou worries about his project, and we worry right along with him. He fears that the epic is slipping out of his grasp and that narration is giving way to dissertation under his pen. He is troubled by the possibility that his remembrance may have succumbed to mythification. Near the end of the book, he confesses resignedly, 'My project was teetering on the brink of failure.'

It is only fair to note, however, that Bénabou has spoken to us all along in the conditional mode, telling us how his book *might* have been written if only he had been equal to the task. At every moment, his writing strains toward that virtual book through a dynamic of hypothesis, speculation, and intense longing. Moreover, in suggesting to us how that ideal book might come to be, his own book comes into being, felicitously and superbly. A tenuous but very wonderful eventuality occurs to him finally: perhaps he can turn the impossible book into 'a genuine literary genre with its own norms and rules.' *Mirabile dictu!* For in fact *Jacob, Menahem, and Mimoun: A Family Epic* performs just that sort of literary alchemy. It is in such a perspective, too, where Bénabou's suspicion that 'one always writes the same book' is most amply confirmed, because that alchemic gesture, more than anything else, is what his writing has always *been about.*

Jacob, Menahem, and Mimoun

TO JACOB, MENAHEM, AND MIMOUN,
AND TO THEIR DESCENDENTS,
IN BELATED HOMAGE

*We stutter our thoughts for a long time
before finding the right expression,
just as children stutter their words
before they can say every letter.*
– Joseph Joubert, *Carnets*

INCIPIT

Saturday mornings were always sunny, and I think there have never been, since that time, days as radiant as those.

More than thirty years ago that sentence, as grandiloquent and naive as one could hope to find (but it didn't seem that way to me at the time), was scribbled in the middle of a blank page. A minuscule event, which took place under circumstances I still remember with surprising precision.

It is toward the end of a winter morning, around mid-February. It's cold – much colder than usual – in the École Normale's long, high-ceilinged reading room, which is always inadequately heated. I am sitting, as I do every day, at the second table on the right; thus I am as close as possible to the shelves on which are collected by the hundreds, in an order whose logic seems to me mysterious to say the least, the works devoted to Roman archaeology and history. For the past several months, this has been my place. A narrow territory, marked by a pile of volumes of various sizes, which hardly vary from one week to the next, so slowly am I progressing in my work. I chose this place in the first days following the beginning of the school year in October because it was across from a large bank of windows looking out on the trees of the inner courtyard, and this allows me, even amid the most serious books, not to forget completely the changing of the seasons.

Contrary to what usually happens, I have not been interrupted at all. Not a single one of my fellow students has come in, bearing a few of those bits of news that just can't wait, and which justify breaking, for a moment or two, the rule of silence that reigns in this virtual sanctuary. No conversation, then, about the events of the day, in which our little group takes an anxious interest; the nightmare of the war in Algeria is approaching its end, and we feel, all of us, directly affected by its final bloody spasms. But neither have there been any sophisticated commentaries, whispered under our breath, concerning the films seen yesterday at one of the two theaters to which we go, almost ritually, at least once a day. So that after more than two hours of solitary effort I begin to understand more clearly the long fragment from Apuleius's *Apology* that I have been trying to translate for the past two days. Full of unexpected humor, it has given me great pleasure: it is a resonant hymn in praise of mirrors, accompanied by a few very erudite reflections. Rereading it a final time, I have decided to extract from it, for later use, two brief passages, which I immediately copy out: 'What harm is there, then, in knowing one's own image? . . . Don't you know that for a man there is nothing more worth looking at than his face?' I have to admit that I am particularly fond of Apuleius: with a few others, such as Tertullian (in spite of his excessive ardor) and St. Augustine, whom I at once saw as brothers by virtue of the fact that they were Africans, Romans, and writers, he is part of the little pantheon – wholly personal and secret – that I am constructing for myself on the margins of the values common to our group.

Suddenly the sky, across which a few wispy clouds were still floating, cleared, swept clean by a strong gust of wind. The window, in spite of the slight layer of dust that permanently dims it, lets through a long ray of sunlight: it strikes my eyes obliquely, forcing me to interrupt my reading and lift my head; then it lingers on the bridge of my nose and tickles my upper neck, arousing an agreeable but fleeting sensation of warmth. It is at that moment that, without knowing why, in a tiny, jerky hand, hardly legible, and on a thin, blank sheet hastily drawn from a folder still lying wide open, I write:

Saturday mornings were always sunny, and I think there have never been, since that time, days as radiant as those.

This sentence remained like that for a long time, lost among my notes on the Latin literature of Africa. Not long enough, however, to be altogether forgotten. And when, a few months later, I came across it again, not entirely by chance, a decision at once forced itself on me: it is this sentence, and no other, that should be placed at the beginning of the Book, that book I had been planning for several months and of which a few slender fragments had already been more or less composed.

As the months went on, this sentence was followed, in accord with inspirations as capricious as they were contradictory, by many other sentences intended to accompany it, to support it, to serve it as a triumphal cortege. But no matter how hard I tried, these newcomers always had, in my view, the same defect: they seemed not to be up to the level of that first one, which remained irremediably without kin. As if it involved taking a path, that of nostalgia for the past, which my mind refused to take; as if the intrusion of those distant Sabbath mornings and their miraculous luminosity had been enough to jam, for a long time, at least one part of the mechanism of writing.

I succeeded, later on, in carrying other literary projects through to completion. But in none of them was it possible to inscribe this founding sentence in the place that had been marked out for it ever since its first appearance. So I kept it, all these years, to myself. Like a fetish.

I was sure that some day it would finally be useful.

VOCATION

Exoriare aliquis nostris ex ossibus ultor
[Let an avenger arise from our bones]
– Virgil, *The Aeneid* 4.625

Ja, die Frühlinge brauchten dich wohl. Es mutete manche
Sterne dir zu, dass du sie spürtest. Es hob
sich eine Woge heran im Vergangenen, oder
da du vorüberkamst am geöffneten Fenster,
gab eine Geige sich hin. Das alles war Auftrag,
Aber bewältigtest du's?

[Yes, the springtimes probably needed you. Many stars turned
toward you, so you might mark them. There rose up
a wave flowing out of the past, or else,
as you passed by the open window,
the strains of a violin. This was all a mission,
But were you up to it?]
– Rainer Maria Rilke, *Duineser Elegien*, I

I have never felt comfortable talking about a vocation.

In my view, it is an ambiguous word, frequently used incorrectly, without much concern about its value, when it is not simply confused with various other honored neighbors. Dictionaries, even the most learned, get mixed up on this subject. They lump together, abusively describing them as synonyms, words as different as 'ability,' 'disposition,' 'aptitude,' 'talent,' 'penchant,' 'inclination,' 'taste,' 'faculty,' and indeed, on occasion, 'genius' or 'destiny.' It's enough to give vertigo to a poor wretch trying to find, among this bric-a-brac, the word that could be applied to his case, that could designate the process that has made him precisely what he is.

At the age of twenty, twenty-one perhaps, or a little later (and I couldn't say, I admit, whether or not these are 'the best years of our lives,' no matter what might once have been said on this delicate subject by a fiery young man who ostensibly spent his time, for reasons that concerned him alone, exhaling his anger, and who, saturated as he might have been with a culture drawn from the best classical sources, still seemed not to know – but unfortunately he was not given the time to discover it – that an assertion of this kind, if it is to have any chance of being right, can be advanced only retrospectively and as late as possible, when, as life approaches its end, one finally has at one's disposal the indispensable elements for making a comparison), at the age of twenty, then, twenty-one perhaps, I still did not know what my vocation was, or what it might be. The very sense of the word seemed to me already floating: as floating, I said in an attempt to make those around me smile, as the ship representing Paris on its coat of arms, or the nocturnal breezes over Gilgal.

Others, not far from me, who were leaving without regret or melancholy an interminable adolescence, ready to engage, like real professionals, in the 'business of living' (for which, by virtue of some fortunate atavism, they seemed clearly better prepared than I was), had essentially resolved this problem. I saw them gathering in little closed groups, on mild May evenings, under the trees of the École Normale's inner courtyard: taking as their models all the glorious elders with whom they had no difficulty in identifying, they laughed as they divided up among themselves the great university disciplines, along with a few high positions, captured along the way, in diplomacy, journalism, or administration. To be sure, these were still only imaginary moves up the social ladder. But everyone knew in his heart that these imagined promotions were in all likelihood merely anticipations of the reality to come – which a simple glance, today, at the directory of the Rue d'Ulm's graduates suffices to confirm.

Nothing was preventing me from doing the same. With a few restrictions, the field of possibilities was as open to me as to the others. But I made little effort to cultivate it. These 'careers,' since this word, which then seemed to me to have such an ugly sound, cannot ultimately be avoided, all left me equally cold. I never much liked the idea of 'having a specialty': it seemed to me that my whole being would rebel against what would amount to a mutilation. One of my great pleasures was, on the contrary, to navigate among the disciplines, to make only incongruous conjunctions, to locate only unsuspected relationships. I was convinced that among many apparently disparate phenomena, common structures or mechanisms still remained to be discovered. This mental disposition had colored the whole of my relationship to the things I was studying; in my view, the slightest metaphor was the bearer of a truth that had only to be teased out, the slightest legend was rich with a fragment of history.

And then, most of these specialties, at least the ones that could lead to university professorships, had something in common: they presupposed an extreme attention to the writings and utterances of others. Accepting that obligation would certainly have corresponded in part to my predilections, which were leading me to desire a life devoted to language, to analyses, to more or less learned decipherings. I could not resign myself, however, to accepting this obligation. I saw in it an obstacle to, or a restraint on, another, equally strong desire. Because I had been, for years, anxiously concerned with other people's opinion, I found myself now tortured by a curious itch: to become again, as I had once been, not a person who speaks about others, but one about whom others speak.

This began by chance. I was only ten years old, and we had just moved into what we long called the 'new house.' I had been familiar with the place for ages; I had formed the habit of going there in the afternoon, after school was out, accompanied by one or two friends, whom I took pride in showing around the construction site; then we went to play hide-and-seek among the big piles of stones, split-open bags of sand or cement, trowels and shovels, spirit levels and plumblines. I had been able, week after week, to observe the progress – too slow to suit my mother – of the work, to witness the birth of the different spaces that were going to provide the framework of our family life. Each room had been conceived with its future occupant in mind, and I already knew that none of them had been immediately intended for me, that I would have to wait a bit. Thus, all during the year after we moved in, I slept in my parents' room. It was very long, surrounded on one side – the one closest to the street – by the small, blue living room, where the imposing copper samovar stood majestically enthroned, and on the other side – the one closest to the garden – by the bathroom. My bed had been placed in the far corner (on the living room side), along the end wall, whereas my parents' bed occupied the other corner, across from the window that looked out over the garden. The two beds, which did not face in the same direction, were thus separated by almost the whole length of the room, and in this space had been placed a voluminous, tall, mirrored armoire with three doors. This arrangement allowed the invention of a little stratagem to which I attached a great deal of importance.

As soon as the sun began to filter through the shutters, my father, who always got up early, awoke. At the same moment, activated by some unknown mechanism, my eyes opened. I immediately closed them again. For although I was proud that I could, by a sort of reflex, awaken at exactly the same time as my father, and experience as he did the morning's chilly silence and the sudden irruption of the sparrows' song in the garden, this pride remained interior. I avoided drawing attention to myself by any sign whatever. On the contrary, I did my best to pretend that I was asleep, taking care not to rustle or move the heavy, rather coarse woolen blankets that I had rolled around my shivering body during the night. I put my limbs and especially my head in the exact position that seemed to me to indicate the deepest slumber. I had a single objective: to stay awake, attentive, while I was thought to be asleep. Protected by this simulated sleep, I enjoyed the intoxicating feeling that I had finally realized, at least in part, one of my most cherished dreams: being invisible. Yes – long before I had read H. G. Wells, I had been very strongly affected and persistently haunted by this fantasy of invisibility. Nothing was, in my view, more desirable than being able, at any moment and at will, to vanish, to melt magically into the background, to disappear, while being fully aware that I was nonetheless there. I imagined with delectation all the brave deeds, and also all the practical jokes, that such an ability would make possible. But what most attracted me was the fact that with this marvelous faculty I would be capable of listening, when the opportunity presented itself, to what was said about me. My morning ploy had quickly proven efficacious. To my great satisfaction. I was not there to spy on others, to learn some secret that they wanted to keep from me. I only wanted to be sure that even when I was absent, I did indeed continue to exist in my parents' words: that seemed to me simultaneously reassuring and exciting. The simple utterance of my first name, in the most banal of sentences, was already enough to make my heart beat faster. And when I overheard whole conversations . . .

I would have liked to continue this little game still longer: other people's words, overheard without their knowing it, seemed to me surely the best and most reliable instruments for knowing myself. But on this point, I admit, my wishes were not really fulfilled over the following years. No more than a few scraps of sentences caught here and there: first in my family, and then, a little later, in the lycée, in remarks made by my teachers or by my classmates. These were usually the most anodyne comments, and even when they were not unfavorable to me (and this did happen, sometimes), they always disappointed me a bit: they did not afford me any of the revelations concerning myself, the dazzling illuminations which I patiently, obstinately continued (and still continue) to hope for. I was therefore, as the time of my entry into adulthood approached, far from being satisfied: none of the options that presented themselves seemed likely to lead to the realization of my old fantasy. Could I give up in advance all the gossip, all the commentaries of which I would have liked to be the object and accept what would have been for me, as I strongly felt, a frustration? Therefore I postponed making a choice. Not a very courageous decision, and one which had another defect: it left me facing a great inner void. I found at first various expedients (no point in listing them here) for filling this void. Without, however, being able to make these expedients yield all the joys I was counting on.

In short, I began to get bored.

A new situation, for which I was unprepared: I had never before experienced boredom. Hence I did not know what to make of mine, nor, above all, how to deal with it. Should I take it seriously? Get ready to travel a long way with this new companion? I would have liked to know more precisely its nature. Was it – as I hoped *in petto* – a boredom of superior quality? Might it be comparable to the ones that set you, almost inevitably if you knew how to cultivate them elegantly, on the path to great art? The answer would require a genuine descent into my self, an unlimited exploration. I undertook it. But I made, while doing so, other discoveries. I learned that what was bothering me was the profusion, the fertility, the hypertrophy of memory. Or rather the tyranny of this memory, encumbered by a Moroccan past that refused to pass away, over my relation to reality.

The situation struck me at the time as unjust, and rather paradoxical. For in the course of my last two years in Morocco, which were also the last two years of the Protectorate, I had encountered an exactly parallel state of affairs. I had already discovered how much my perception of things was sometimes biased. This first adulteration was the most tangible result of the education I had received: I had been taught – and this was far from unusual in colonial countries – a history without any connection to my true forebears (the notorious phrase 'Our ancestors the Gauls' was in this domain only the most visible – and not the most harmful or risible[1] – part of a much more devastating whole), a geography that did not in any way correspond to the natural environment in which I was immersed, political principles that were not (by any stretch of the imagination!) those current in the society in which I was living. I had absorbed all that in large doses and with considerable appetite, without any concern other than that of getting good marks, deferring questions, silencing the worries that sometimes surged up from contradictions that were too glaring. Little by little, people, landscapes, and ways of life that had no concrete link with me had taken up residence in my mind and in my dreams, and acquired the status of unsurpassable models. I thus moved, much of the time, in a largely imaginary universe. Even the street names, signs on shops, and the brands of the products we bought, most of which referred, with a rather monotonous insistence, to the provinces, mountains, and cities or rivers of France, contributed to the maintenance of this phantasmal geography from which I was unable to extirpate myself. If during a walk I happened to glimpse, on a street or restaurant sign, words such as *Normandie, Bourgogne,* or *Bretagne,* I immediately felt how intensely I missed this Brittany, Burgundy, or Normandy, which were so close to my heart, so well known to my memory, and where I had never set foot. (I could have hummed, with very ecumenical conviction, 'Oh qu'elle est belle ma Bretagne', 'Je veux revoir ma Normandie', 'Et je suis fier d'être bourguignon', since, not being from any province, I could claim them all.) Thus a veritable restructuring of my senses had gradually been carried out. The values incul-

[1]. I would even add that it stopped seeming risible at all a few years later, when I consented to see in it not a literal truth, but a figurative expression of an intellectual relationship. Since I was caught up in the same history as the descendants of the Gauls, since I was prepared to share their future, what was so ridiculous about espousing, at least metaphorically, their past?

cated at school and by reading stayed with me, and continued to organize most of my reactions. Everything that lay before my eyes had mysteriously lost its value; whence a more or less permanent feeling of nostalgia mixed with frustration. My desire to leave Morocco, to close the gap that separated me from what I cherished, arose in part from this feeling.

And now that I found myself on French soil, where this hiatus was supposed to be wiped out, where immediate perception and imaginary constructions could at last come together – and even (what joy!) exactly coincide – I encountered the most unforeseen, most surprising, most absurd of obstacles: it was the Moroccan past that now inopportunely interposed itself! Minor incidents, which I had not even noticed when I was living through them, reappeared. As if some evil genius, who had at first sought to divert them from my consciousness and collect them in an invisible container, henceforth took pleasure in releasing them in successive volleys. Thus I discovered that my Moroccan years – seventeen in all and no more, but the first seventeen – had deposited in me, in packed strata, a gigantic mass of memories which, constantly ready to surge up with a dimension and relief I had not known they possessed, gave everything I was experiencing in Paris a very peculiar shape and coloration.

Thus the simple cup of coffee I drank every day (a postprandial rite I had at first had trouble getting used to, but which I had adopted, along with many others, after only a few weeks), in the smoky Café Soufflot or in the Bar des Ursulines, inevitably brought back, somewhere deep within my nostrils, the familiar but now absent perfume of the big glass of mint tea, brewed and sugared just right, which my father made every day following the afternoon nap, with his customary precision, and which he liked to sip silently with me, in the garden, before beginning Minkha, the afternoon prayer. In the same way, a quick meal, eaten Saturday between noon and one o'clock on the noisy and poorly heated terrace of a Boul' Mich' restaurant (it was almost always a cafeteria, La Source or else Le Capoulade, which had not yet been swallowed up by the recent wave of merchants selling sausages or hamburgers), immediately evoked the memory, still quite vivid, of our robust Sabbath dinners, their ceremony, and the minuscule events to which this weekly celebration gave rise. We had to wait, before sitting down to table in the patio (that was what we called the large central room), for the whole family to assemble. There were often, among my brothers, latecomers. As soon as the last one to arrive had taken his place, my father began the recitation of the psalms and prayers for that day, while my mother went into the kitchen to make her indispensable last-minute preparations: checking the seasoning of the half-dozen hors d'oeuvres she had made the preceding day, sprinkling a bit of cumin on the beets or eggplants, a few drops of lemon juice on the big red grilled peppers. But of course she took care to be present at the most important moment, when the wine and the bread were blessed. That is why my father had formed the habit, when he arrived at the verse that preceded each of these blessings, of pointedly raising his voice and slowing his delivery, pronouncing separately and with care each of the familiar Hebrew syllables ('Ka-a-mur po-te-yah et ya-dé-kha'). My mother, thus warned, hurried back. But sometimes, her tasks in the kitchen having taken longer than she had anticipated, she was a little slow in responding to this coded message. Everyone then remained in suspense, and in the heavy silence my father had to hold on the tip of his tongue the last words of the prayer. Which always put him in a rather foul humor: he didn't like to wait. Fortunately, once the milestone of the blessings had been passed, and the first hors d'oeuvres were put on the table, the usual family hubbub started up again.

And, alone in this city where I found the streets without odor, fruit without taste, and Saturdays without sun, mechanically dipping in mustard the lukewarm and cardboard-like fries overflowing onto my meal tray, I tried to recover, somewhere at the back of my palate, something of the savor of my mother's potatoes, which fifteen hours of cooking over a low fire in a mixture of meat, chick peas, wheat, and aromatic spices had filled to the bursting point with a thick and yet fluid, beautifully caramel-colored sauce.

Sometimes, in order to keep the memory from becoming too importunate, I preferred not to wait until it manifested itself: I tried to head it off by anticipating its appeals. I believed that in this way I would have a better chance of controlling it. But the result of my naive ruses was seldom what I expected. Thus the fritters and almond-paste confections that I went to devour in a Tunisian pastry shop near the Rue Saint-Séverin (I had not found, at that time, any Moroccan equivalent in the Latin Quarter), as a remedy for the melancholy that afflicted me on wintry Sunday evenings, just before I had to return, in the rain, to the dormitory at the Lycée Louis-le-Grand: right from the first bite, swallowed each time with the same gluttonous impatience (as if I were sure that the miracle was finally going to occur), I was disenchanted. I found the fritters lukewarm or pasty, and in the so-called almond-paste, the rancid taste of the peanuts that had been abundantly – and improperly – mixed in was too obvious. Instead of being calmed, the sensation of loss grew even more vivid. And my thoughts were also occupied by the hot, light, voluminous, crackling fritters eaten on certain September mornings after a night spent in pious reading, or again by the exquisite almond confections (little rolls in the form of cigars, big stuffed dates, macaroons, gazelle horns) which returned unchanged, several times a year, to enchant our countless family reunions. As for my experiences, later on, with certain 'Moroccan restaurants' (a denomination that really ought to be more strictly limited), and their tajines, mechouis, kefta, or couscous, I would just as soon, even now, not discuss them.

It had not been necessary for me to read ethnology in order to learn that certain cultural characteristics – especially those having to do with eating habits – remain buried for a long time without being affected by changes in their surroundings; but I did not know that their persistence could take the form of such a brutal irruption of memory. I also discovered that my active, overzealous, excessively energetic memory was not – as in the case of so many other people whose attitude I at first found more or less stimulating – a victory over time, a miraculous restitution, in identical form, of fragments of the past, a renewal of buried happiness; on the contrary, by interfering with the present, all it did was rob the moment I was living of most of its delight.

I had to accept the obvious: Morocco stuck to my memory, as if the bonds that attached me to that land refused to break. I, who had just recently gotten off the boat at Marseilles, and was then bounced around during an interminable train trip that took me to Paris; who had vowed to visit systematically all the museums, cloisters, and châteaus, all the cathedrals, churches, chapels, crypts, and medieval towers for which there were signs as one came into every tiny village in France – I was literally hobbled by memory. But that had nothing to do with the lyricism of sea and sun that had spread superficially during the fifties among some readers of Camus, or with the nostalgia for Mediterranean insouciance that was to mark, much later on, the literature of those who returned to France from Algeria.

Instead of being distressed by the strangeness of my situation, I should have meditated on Goethe's judicious precept: 'The man who has a good memory should not envy anyone.' In fact, I believe that when I first arrived in France, I did not envy anyone. Sometimes I even felt a certain compassion for those of my friends whom I saw confined within the superficiality of a rather gray present; if I had known, at that time, the adjective *one-dimensional*, it is the one I would have used to describe them. I went around wearing a little smile of indulgence, and occasionally of irony.

It seemed to me a shame not to go further. After all, I had an advantage, and I was not yet making sufficient use of it. So much past being present ought to be of some help in constructing a future for myself! Why not try to mobilize it in the service of the 'intellectual aptitudes' that people readily saw in me, and which I considered as still largely unused? Once formulated, this suggestion was soon transformed into an imperative.

The schema might well seem hackneyed: recourse to the past, a classical way of getting around a blocked present. It nonetheless seemed to me original, since in this case it was memory that was responsible for the blockage, and since, by way of writing, the emergence of the past would cease to be the illness and become instead the remedy. Hence one evening, on the way back from the cinema to the Rue d'Ulm (I had just seen three Russian films in succession, including Pudovkin's *Mother*), I made a solemn resolution, which I wrote down in the big spiral-bound notebook where I recorded important matters: I was going to *channel, discipline my memory's overflows by giving them a literary form.* In my view, this formulation had the advantage of being neutral; it allowed me to avoid expressions such as 'autobiography,' 'memoirs,' or 'narrative of childhood,' the very utterance of which, at that time, made my hackles rise. What I wanted was to hit at least three targets with a single stone: to put my memory into sentences (which I had moreover also called 'transforming my experience into language') in order to rid myself of the excess of untimely recollections; to make more effective use of a much too idle present; and finally to guarantee me a more stimulating future. I was only too happy to be able to give the name 'vocation' to this imperative, which then began to exercise its pressure on me with the persistence of a true idée fixe, and I realized that for a long time it was going to define the framework of my activities.

This first step, even though it was not immediately followed by any other, made it possible for me to regain my footing. But I soon perceived, by ruminating on it, that my embryonic literary project could have a utility far greater than the one I had at first attributed to it, which was hardly more than therapeutic and moreover colored by a strong dose of narcissism. If I were able to direct it in the right way, it would also help me 'acquit myself' with regard to my own people, my family as well as the community from which I sprang: I was going to have an opportunity to liquidate at one stroke all my pending debts! For I had very early on had the feeling that I was loaded down with a great number of debts, involuntarily contracted from my birth onward, and never paid.

This had become apparent, in a way I had never expected, with my discovery of what had really happened in the Second World War. Thanks to Morocco's distance from Europe, thanks to the courageous attitude of the sultan, who refused to ratify the anti-Semitic measures imposed by the extremely 'Vichyist' General Noguès, thanks finally to the American landing in 1942, the war was not, for the Jewish community in Morocco, the catastrophe that it was elsewhere. From this period I had retained only the most distant impressions. The strongest presented itself this way: someone – no doubt my mother – is trying to make me swallow something – some medicine, apparently – that I reject very vehemently. Very early on, I had put this impression of nausea in relation with another memory, that of the typhus epidemic that has erupted during a particularly torrid summer (1943, probably); that summer, to avoid contagion, it was indispensable to take every day some little yellow tablets that had an extraordinarily bitter taste; I agreed to swallow them, against my will, only when they were put in a large mouthful of orange marmalade (a similar expedient was used, a little later, to get me to ingurgitate my daily spoonful of cod-liver oil). Concerning the war proper, nothing very tragic had been engraved on my memory: the periodic growling of the sirens, which didn't seem to worry people in the neighborhood much; the numerous parallel trenches dug not far from our house, in the courtyard of the school for boys, but which I don't recall ever having gotten into; the big sheets of blue paper stuck to the windowpanes to camouflage, at dusk, the feeble electric light. Besides that, as if to correct these (moderately) negative impressions, a few clearly pleasant moments: the surprise appearances, in the main street of our neighborhood (the one we always called 'the boulevard'), of American soldiers – tall and blond, but also sometimes, to my great astonishment, black; the children swarming and shoving around the jeeps and trucks of these visitors who were always welcome; the treats they handed out (candy, wafers, chocolates, and the inevitable chewing gum), laughing heartily. I knew, moreover – and I was very proud of this – that some of my uncles and cousins from Rabat had been sent to Europe to fight against the Germans: a photograph of one of them, smiling in his uniform, had a place of honor in the family album, graced with an indecipherable dedication. In addition to all that, there was, finally, a particularly precise recollection (the most precise of all those concerning this period), the recollection of the night victory was announced, 8 May 1945: the neighborhood streets were plunged into darkness as a result of a power outage (this happened often);

the 'new synagogue' (which, it seems to me, I was entering for the first time, wearing an enormous Basque beret), lit only by a few oil lamps and packed with people; at the end of the prayer, a long, long walk, my father holding my hand and forced at times to drag me along because I had difficulty keeping up with him; around us, everywhere, a dense, excited crowd composed of young and old mixed up together; in the middle of 'the boulevard,' a knot of people; a mustachioed effigy being burned at the foot of an electric pole; a few young men brandishing flaming torches; others loudly chanting 'Hitler-to-the-stake!' About this tragic period, that is about all that has remained in my memory.

Hence my surprise when I began to be informed as to the reality of what had occurred. In particular when I saw for the first time, in a movie theater, what June 1940 had been like for France: the collapse, the debacle, the exodus, the occupation. Very soon, unbearable images, especially those of columns of haggard refugees being bombarded (these have since become classics of memory), began to haunt me. I couldn't get over the fact that such a thing could have happened, not in a distant past, as in my history books, but virtually in the present, when I was already in this world; especially, I couldn't get over the fact that I had escaped it.

Then I began to read things on Nazism, on the deportation, on the death camps. I had not the slightest conception of these things, for around me they were never mentioned. They were revealed to me fortuitously. It happened a few months after we had moved. Joyfully, I took possession of the room, at the far end of the garden, which was to become 'my office,' but which in fact I shared with my sister Anne. I had decided to arrange, in alphabetical order, on the long bookshelves of unpainted wood I had asked my father to install, all the books I had been able to collect, so that finally, I too could have at my disposal the magical object the desire for which had already obsessed me for years: a genuine 'library'! While I was putting my books in order, I came across two pamphlets. Their bindings were in bad shape, and I was not able to find the authors' names, so I didn't know where to put them. But their strange titles had interested me enough to make me to look through them, and then read them. One was called *The Hell at Treblinka,* and the other *Drancy the Jewess.* I read them feverishly, with growing agitation: I was discovering, suddenly and almost simultaneously, the Nazis and their French collaborators. I was stupefied. To the point that I dared not speak about it to anyone around me, not even to those of my brothers I normally told everything. It was as if I had violated, involuntarily, a dreadful secret. I wondered how such books could have found their way into our house, and I hoped, against all logic, that no member of the family had happened to look at them; I preferred not even to imagine the effect the least of these pages would have had on my mother! In fact, I wished, with all my heart, that no one in the world might know that 'that' – I could find no name for it – had been able to exist. This feeling was soon accompanied by an uneasiness, difficult to define, that crystallized in a troubled question: how would *I* have reacted, had I been involved in 'that'? A lacerating question that was eventually transformed into another that bore more directly on the present: how was I to respond to the fact that I had not had to endure 'that,' while so many others, who were no more guilty than I was, had been subjected to it? I had gradually persuaded myself that I had been the beneficiary of a kind of miracle, in any case, of a genuine stroke of luck. But what had I done to deserve that luck, or that miracle? And above all, what must I do to continue to be worthy of it? I had been pursued by this anguished concern. Sometimes it seemed to abate, during long periods of remission. But revived by the sporadic resurgences –

in more or less acknowledged forms – of Nazism and anti-Semitism, it never had a chance to die out entirely.

Such was the first of my 'debts.' It weighed on me all the more because I had always kept it secret, not having found anyone to whom I could talk about it, or anyone who could tell me to whom I owed it.

The second debt was wholly different. I was well aware, in this case, who held the IOUs. No one other than my parents. Because they incarnated, along with a few other people of their generation, a rather singular assortment of qualities: an attachment to the old morality, somewhat austere, in which they had been raised (an attachment based on the conviction that respect for divine commandments is necessary for the maintenance of the world order); an aptitude for injecting a dose of the sacred into even the smallest corners of everyday life, thus giving family life, especially on Holy Days, a savor I have never found again; finally, as the main reason for living, a complete devotion to their children's interest. All this had provided, despite a few privations, a fairly enviable environment for my earliest childhood years.

I had, because of propitious circumstances, both historical (the return, at the end of the war, of a relative prosperity) and familial (my position as the next-to-youngest of eight children), benefited from parental attention more than some of my elder siblings, who had had to endure the full impact of the war's repercussions. Moreover, through contacts with some of my friends, through listening to things they sometimes told me about their own family lives, I had gradually become aware of how privileged my situation had been. And this situation was further prolonged when my elder siblings, in turn, started to add their own coddling to that of my parents. Thus from my adolescence onward I dreamed, in a confused sort of way, of some striking act that would allow me to demonstrate my gratitude for everything that had been given me.

All the more since, as I was well aware, the direction my life was taking, toward resolutely 'profane' activities, was not exactly the one that would have fully satisfied my parents. To be sure, they had never expressed any wish regarding my professional future or that of my brothers, other than to see us 'succeed,' or 'be happy,' without saying precisely what they meant by that, and so our freedom to choose was left more or less untrammeled. I imagined the difficulties, the intimate contradictions they had had to overcome in order to arrive at that point: they had had to maintain as rigorously as possible the body of traditions, essentially religious, that had constituted, from generation to generation, the family's strength, and at the same time to let in enough fresh air so that each child could take the best advantage of the new order of things (marked by 'Europeanization'). But they had nonetheless retained some of their old dreams, and sometimes let them filter through in signs that did not leave much room for doubt.

Thus, to fulfill their desire, I, the last of their male children, should have incarnated at least one of the roles they considered noblest, that of the rabbi. They saw me, of course, as a 'chief rabbi,' with all that assumed in the way of mastery of sacred knowledge, exemplary piety, and social prestige. One of those learned men of whom there are only a few in each generation and who could be instantly recognized. Round hat with a broad scarlet brim, a flowing beard (like that of a postcard Santa Claus), delicate complexion, fine white hands, an ample black robe falling to the ankles – they had a charisma that affected everyone. My mother had known at least one of them in her youth, Rabbi Yehoshua (Berdugo), who had been the chief rabbi of Morocco. The strong personality and openness of mind of this exceptional man had made a lasting impression on her. Ever since, she had shown an almost religious respect for these qualities, which was equaled only by the respect she was later to show for 'men of knowledge' in general, and for physicians in particular. Yes: what would have satisfied her, since her status as a woman did not allow her to accede to these heights herself, would have been to come as close to them as possible. She, who had always loyally conformed to all the expectations that were incumbent upon her as a wife and Jewish mother, hoped that some day her merits would be recognized: what better reward than to become the mother of a master to whom people listened, who was capable of inspiring in everyone a fear of God, love for the Law, and respect for the Commandments?

But I had not followed the pious path, had not climbed the traditional steps. And so I could read only with great difficulty, and without understanding much, the classical commentaries of the French rabbi Rashi, whose text, with its minuscule, rounded letters, contrasted strongly with the squared-off Hebrew of the Torah, which it accompanied like its shadow. I had never taken up seriously the study of the *dinim* (laws), and still less the infinite exploration of the exegetes and commentators that crowded into the intimidating pages of the Gemara and the Mishnah. In short, there was little chance that I would someday honor my parents by improvising, in some thorny Talmudic debate, one of the novel interpretations that marked the birth of a new master. In fact, whatever my fervor in other regards (and it was great when I was about ten years old), my relations with religious teaching continued to be difficult.

I had never taken to the rabbinical school, the one we called Talmud Torah. I went there at least four (or even five) years in a row, for about two months each year, during the summer; thus it occupied a large part of my vacation time, and I can say without hesitation that the hours I spent there were among the least pleasant of my childhood.

The building itself, standing like a sentinel at the edge of the neighborhood, just across from the wall of the old cemetery, had nothing inviting about it: a heavy square structure that, with its raised main floor and the two stories above it, seemed enormous amid the uniformly low houses around it. Inside, on each side of the square, classrooms. In the middle, a tiled courtyard, without a blade of grass, where there could be no question of running or playing, for it was barely large enough to hold the hundreds of students during the all-too-rare recreation periods. There I felt a sensation of being closed in whose equivalent I experienced only much later, and to my great surprise, when I found myself, for the first time, in the courtyard of the Lycée Louis-le-Grand in Paris.

And then, the process that took me to the rabbinical school every year, at the beginning of July, weighed on me. The difference from the Alliance Israélite school, where I was following the standard program (which imitated, with the exception of a few details, the French model), with teachers who were often friends of my brothers and sisters, was really too great. The last days of the year there were by far the most charming. The courses got less demanding, we spent our time in games, amusements, and delights of all kinds. But above all, we celebrated the coming arrival of the summer vacation with a joyful burst of rounds and songs ('Gai, gai, l'écolier, c'est demain les vacances'), which we caroled tirelessly under the window of the principal, who showed a less severe countenance during that time. Then the school closed. A torrid wind came to transform the city into a furnace. Then, like all my friends, I thought only of shade, coolness, and the countless pleasures of our beloved municipal swimming pool.

In spite of its somewhat segregationist rules (admission to the pool, which was open to all during the week, was reserved for Muslims on Fridays, for Jews on Saturday, and for Christians on Sunday), and in spite of the terrible crush that occurred at closing time, when you had to fight your way into the dressing room to collect your damp, wrinked clothes, the pool became, as soon as the first hot days arrived – that is, as soon as the Easter vacation was over – the object of all our desires, for we spent all our leisure time there. I would have liked to go on spending my mornings or afternoons there with my little group of friends. I loved our interminable running from one pool to another, or our diving contests, with the enormous plumes that each of our dives raised; you just had to try to avoid the eye of Allel, the vigilant head lifeguard, whose tall, muscled silhouette, handsomely shining black in the sunlight, ruled imperially over the whole place. We stopped our play, our lips blue and our eyes red, only when we were truly exhausted. A very frugal snack, or a short nap on the grass, in the shade of a mulberry tree, whose fruit sometimes fell softly on our faces, and we began again.

Sadly, a morning always came when I had to give up these incomparable delights. It happened at the beginning of the week, that is, one Sunday. My mother announced in a sweet but resolute voice that the time to return to Talmud Torah had come, explaining at length why I must go there: she probably would have talked about 'the salvation of my soul,' had that expression been used in our house. She told me to put on a shirt, although I would have much preferred to remain, like the rest of the children in the neighborhood, shirtless or wearing only a singlet. Then, unmoved by my begging (usually I claimed I had sudden stomach pains, and these were not even always feigned, imploring her to give me a few days' reprieve), she firmly took my hand in hers and led me away. We made our way through the neighborhood streets, which were silent and sunbeaten, I still sniveling somewhat, she pulling me along and at the same time trying to console me. So as to be in the shade, we walked along the courtyard, and then the façade, of the girls' school; with genuine sadness, I stopped for moment in front of one of the windows, that of the classroom where, during the school year, my elder sister taught her classes (and where I had formed the habit of going to join her, at the end of each morning, to do part of my homework under her tutelage). Next, we passed by the shops in the market. I took advantage of them to stop once again, trying to spot the big straw basket that served as a table for the man who sold Barbary figs; sometimes my mother was indulgent enough to let me eat two or three of them (they were deliciously fresh, the merchant having extracted them from their heavy skins covered with spines with three blows – and not a single one more – of his glistening knife); or else, she allowed me to buy a few pieces of cinnamon bark, which I loved to suck on all day long, like sticks of licorice. The last leg of the trip – the longest and sunniest – unfortunately offered no pretext for stopping: it passed in front of a line of undistinguished houses. We already began to hear the psalmodies, chants, and cries of a multitude of children. Shrill. Dissonant. A cacophony that hurt your ears. We were nearing our goal. A final sob. A last battle – which I knew was already lost – to delay, even for one day, even for just a morning, the fatal hour. Finally, still pulled along by my mother, I went into the intimidating edifice. I had no sooner crossed the threshold than the stomachache I had complained about more or less sincerely as we were leaving the house became a sad – and undeniable – reality. I would have liked to run away to take refuge a moment in the toilets; but even that ultimate and absurd escape hatch was forbidden me; the odor that emanated from that place would have forced me to beat a hasty retreat before I had gotten anywhere near the door . . .

What awaited me next I knew all too well: an anguishing route I would have preferred not to follow again. The first hurdle was the 'examination.' This took place in the office of the rabbi-director, which was overflowing with Hebrew books of all sizes and formats (many of them lay open, piled on top of each other). To gauge the level of my knowledge and to decide which way I should go, he abruptly held out a volume (one of the five books of the Torah) and, with an authoritative finger, asked me to try to read a page he had chosen arbitrarily. Petrified with fear and timidity, at first I remained silent; it took me long, long minutes to regain a little assurance and finally succeed in articulating, in a hesitating voice, hardly audible (and without paying any attention to the cantilation signs), the first words of the text: *Vaydaber Adonai el Moshe lemor: dabber el bene Israel veamarta alehem ani Adonai elohekhem* . . . after five or six verses, the august figure rendered his verdict: 'Rabbi Shlomo' or 'Rabbi David.' Immediately, more dead than alive, and my stomach still tied in painful knots, I was led into the class to which I had just been, in such an efficient way, assigned for the rest of the summer. Old teachers – improperly called rabbis – wore themselves out trying to make groups of children as numerous as they were tumultuous swallow, in Hebrew and in Arabic, a few more verses of the Torah. Their pedagogy came down from the beginning of time: it was simply the ancient method of reading a passage in unison, out loud, and tirelessly repeating it until it had been definitively inscribed on every pupil's memory.

The classroom I entered bore no resemblance to the ones in my school: here, there was no dais or desk for the teacher, no colored chalks that crumbled delicately under your fingers, no damp cloth sliding over the blackboard, no world globe, no wall map titled *The Peoples of Gaul,* no engravings picturing *Joan of Arc at the Battle of Orleans, Saint Louis Rendering Decisions under an Oak Tree, The Coronation of the Emperor Napoleon I.* The pupils, exclusively boys, sat on benches without backs, arranged in concentric squares. In the middle stood the rabbi, within reach of a long stick with which he occasionally vigorously struck the most unruly boys. Still stuffy despite their high ceilings and constantly open windows, filled to overflowing with a mob of sweating children, these classrooms emitted, during these weeks of hot weather, an acrid and coarse odor, the memory of which followed me from one summer to the next.

Without real attachment to an institution of which I made only occasional use, I arrived at the rabbinical school with a few big handicaps, with the result that I remained from every point of view, during the whole time I spent there, an intruder. First of all, no matter how archaic the teaching was, I had difficulty in attaining the required level: I could not reasonably expect, in spite of my efforts, to catch up with a class that had already been going on for several months. But above all, I had virtually no interaction with my provisional classmates: we had literally nothing to say to one another. A few of them, whose size and age allowed them to play the rebel's role, were already acting like impertinent adolescents, while I was just a greenhorn, completely unused to a universe in which physical strength, vitality of expression, manual dexterity – especially in spinning tops, or using a sling to hunt sparrows – were the only criteria of superiority.

The last year, however, something changed. Someone other than the usual rabbi-director greeted me at the entrance to the school: short black beard, hat and suit in the European style (which was, for the image I had of rabbis, a small revolution). It was he who, after having subjected me to the ritual brief examination (in which my performance was – I don't know why; it had become familiar, I suppose – a little better), had the idea of sending me not to the boring old scarecrows I had had to endure up to then, but to one of the new teachers who had just been recruited, precisely in order to give a new luster to the institution. Much younger, more 'modern,' he got through the obligatory readings (daily prayers, the weekly passages from the Torah and the Prophets) pretty quickly, giving him time to teach us to speak and write modern Hebrew. I was immediately drawn to this new teaching: the framework and methods now resembled somewhat more those to which I was accustomed. My mistrust with regard to the institution began to melt away, and I even considered, this time without any sort of repulsion, returning there. But it was too late. At the end of the following year I was eleven years old, and I passed the entrance exam for the first year at the Lycée Poeymirau. The time of 'studies' was beginning. My family decided I now had a right to a real vacation. Ifrane (the mountains) or Rabat (the seacoast) replaced Talmud Torah. My rabbinical career went no further.

Thus I had to try to palliate my parents' secret disappointment about this desertion, and – to be pardoned for it – to give them at least, as a way of making amends, a reason for being proud of me in another domain. I did not fail to find significant, and almost premonitory, the fact that they had given me the Hebrew first name of Menahem, which means 'merciful': hadn't they thereby designated for me precisely the role of consoler, which I was someday to play? Thus as soon as I had learned a little about our family history, about its ancient glory (which I regretted not having witnessed firsthand) and its recent setbacks (of which, on the contrary, I had felt the repercussions in the embarassment and penury that had marked certain moments in my childhood), a solution emerged: I persuaded myself that it was up to me to give back to my parents, without quite knowing how I would do it, a little of the luster the cruelly vivid memory of which was still with them. For if my eldest brother, who in the early fifties had become the main pillar of our family, had contributed in a decisive way to our financial recovery, the wound to our pride, which was deeper in my mother than in my father, had not been completely healed. Both of them still bore, in their relations with the world, a tenacious form of disappointment, and even sometimes of resentment. It was up to me to deliver them from this.

But once I had made the decision to assume the role of avenger, there could be no question of stopping there. That would have been to go only halfway! My entirely new function as the dispenser of justice, it seemed to me, had to be expanded far beyond the limits of the family circle, to the benefit of the extended family constituted, in my view, by all the Jews in Morocco. The feeling that I owed them a debt, no less burdensome than the two preceding ones, had an unusual genesis and history. It had appeared later, almost at the end of my adolescence, but it had developed during my first years in Paris, when I discovered, through the questions I was sometimes asked (one of my classmates in the preparatory class for the École Normale had asked me one day if we were 'white'), or through certain little misadventures, the extent to which Moroccan Judaism was unknown, or worse yet, misunderstood. Just one example: the first time I entered into contact with a group of Jewish students, in a small, poorly furnished meeting place near the Luxembourg Garden, there was someone there (the very pretty redhead who was supposed to greet newcomers, and whose big green eyes had immediately struck my heart) who thought it surprising and a bit suspicious that I could not speak a single word in Yiddish. I was outraged, then, to see that this venerable community, which was thousands of years old (I had obviously adopted as unchallengeable truths the old hypotheses according to which Hebrews went to Africa in the time of King Solomon), continued to be seen as insignificant. Even within Sephardic Judaism, which was already marginalized with respect to the major centers of Jewish culture, it was considered a poor relation, a somewhat disgraceful cousin, more often the object of commiseration than of genuine respect: people liked to describe it as leaning on an old-fashioned religious tradition, mixed up with ridiculous superstitions; they jeered cruelly at its immemorial refusal to change. Of its very long history, they were inclined to remember only the darkest periods, in particular the last years before the establishment of the French Protectorate, when poverty, fear, humiliation, and sometimes pillaging and massacres – historical realities that were, moreover, undeniable – seemed to have become the rule. In that way, centuries of intense life, marked by constant exchanges with the rest of the world, rich in successes of all kinds, in original and sometimes exemplary spiritual adventures, remained wholly unknown to almost everyone, even scholars. There were, here and there, a few amateur ethnologists, armed with at most a great condescension with regard to the pitiable object they were studying; but they were content, most of the time, with reducing to a few bazaar clichés, hastily slapped on, the subtleties of a society whose rules of operation essentially eluded them.

I felt myself invested with the duty of battling against this injustice. It was urgent to give the external world, Jews and Gentiles together, which persisted in an ignorance or misunderstanding equally guilty and equally damaging to our honor, a correct image, to provide the keys that would allow the deciphering of a history, a tradition, a patrimony. At a time when other people were undertaking, with a courage that I was glad to salute, the 'decolonization' of their history, wasn't it time to take ours out of the closet where it had been put away? I even hoped to go further yet, and, in this pious task, to benefit from the few prophetic aspects that our community, too long closed up in its ritualistic scruples (and how much we have been reproached for this 'dessicated ritualism'!), had to have hidden away somewhere for the intrepid person who would one day know how to bring them out. They would perhaps allow me, these finally rediscovered prophetic aspects, to restore to my people a lineage of heroes to celebrate in great collective ceremonies. I almost envied – without, however, going so far as to want to emulate – all those who had, elsewhere, been so bold as to rewrite the entire history of humanity, centering it purely and simply on their own people, or even, like that Annius of Viterbo, whose existence I had recently discovered through his prodigious epigraphic falsifications, on their own city. They were all singing their own heroes; should we be the only ones who agreed to remain silent forever?

One final consideration comforted me in my attitude. I still had in mind – and I was far being alone in this at the time – the Sartrian model of commitment. As a future 'intellectual,' I could not without cowardice escape the urgent task of cultural preservation: to save as many vestiges of a world that everything indicated was fragile and ultimately threatened as I could. I saw clearly that after the successives exoduses that had begun in 1948 with the birth of Israel, someday nothing would remain of what had been for centuries our ancestors' way of life. However, I did not suspect that in a few years the process was going to undergo a prodigious acceleration and realize several generations in advance my darkest forebodings.

Thus I had to speak out, I had to put this history, our history, at the center of my universe, I had to love it and work for it alone. Thus, in everything I said, I would be the product of that impulse, the bearer of that communitarian sensibility that had not yet had a chance to attain what from then on represented for me the only acceptable way of being perennial: being translated into French words.

My path seemed to be laid out for me.

Settling my personal accounts, avenging the family, rehabilitating the community – a whole set of external and internal requirements dictated what I had to do. This was no longer a simple caprice on the part of an idle young man, a whim I could treat casually, but rather the logical end result of a history. A written text was necessary, one that would confer on the people and things in my memory an undoubted existence, and even, if I could find the appropriate form, raise them to an entirely new, and much higher, level of existence.

I now knew that so long as I had not acquitted myself of these multiple debts, which in my mind overlapped and reinforced each other, I would go on living the unsatisfied and precarious life that I was no longer completely sure was the one for which I had been born. For while my ruminations, carried along by their own energy and feeding on themselves, continued in this way, I also began to feel looming within myself the possibility of a greater achievement, of higher tasks. After all, the destiny that had strongly seconded my efforts for years, and to which I was already indebted for some judicious nudges, had not yet required anything of me in return. I saw clearly that the objective conditions were favorable to me. No one was better prepared to undertake the project: wasn't I the only one (or almost the only one) who had, with respect to my subject, both the proximity and the distance necessary, the only one who could combine, as the anthropological jargon of the period put it, participatory observation and a distanced perspective?

BOOK

Book: a spiral. – Michel Leiris

*I spent my childhood lying flat
on my stomach, reading books.*
– Victor Hugo

*Blessed are the eyes that
witness these splendors!
When the ear hears the tale,
the soul is filled with sorrow.*
– Extract from the Moussaf
prayer at Yom Kippur

Everything seemed thus to have conspired to make me end up at ... a book. The strict Mallarmean orthodoxy of my procedure, at least on this point, was assured.

This was hardly surprising to me. I had encountered books in all the stages of my life; I should say, to be more precise, that it was my encounters with various kinds of books that had served (and still serve, sometimes) to define the stages of my life. It was to be expected that a book would be the instrument chosen to help me pass into still another stage, perhaps the most important one.

In fact, I was not far from believing that there was in the history of my relationship with books – and with the act of reading – a sort of predestination. Of course, I could explain this by repeating, as so many others have, that I belong to the so-called People of the Book, and let it go at that. But behind these words, which I cannot in good grace refuse to apply to myself, there is for me more than the conventional meaning, which refers to a special link connecting all Jews with the Torah. For me, they refer to an entirely different, everyday relationship with individual books, in their most material reality.

One of the very first books I had in my hands (I dare not claim that it was *the* first) was not one of those picture books with thick pages, filled with brightly colored images, that people think they have to give children to awaken their interest in reading. No, it was a book with a less inviting appearance and a more austere content. In short: a prayerbook. A rather heavy volume, which I could barely hold in my hand, each time I went, on tiptoe, to take it down from the bookcase where it was ordinarily shelved in my parents' bedroom. It impressed me because it was the one my father used for his three daily prayers. But I was also aware of its reassuring qualities: its robust smell, in which there seemed still to be some trace of a lukewarm stew or sweet potatoes cooked in the ashes, its maroon imitation leather binding torn along the spine, where there were always a few threads hanging down, its title half worn away, and its parchmentlike pages, speckled here and there with little grease spots that made them translucent.

It was from this book that I learned to read Hebrew. I had arrived at the age – I'd passed my fifth birthday – when my religious training was to begin. My father, according to tradition and to his own wishes, was supposed to undertake this task, but his work kept him away from the house most of the week. Thus it was my mother who assumed this role. Her competence in the subject was obviously not equal to my father's, but what she knew of Hebrew, which she had studied passionately in her youth – and not without pride, for in her generation it was not the custom to teach Hebrew to daughters – was amply sufficient.

When she started teaching me, she did not know, I think, the old custom that consists in shaping the Hebrew letters in honey and then giving them to the child to eat. In any case, that was not the way she proceeded with me (and I don't regret it). She used this book because it was the one she had at hand and because it could, thanks to its large, black, well-defined characters, play the role of primer. To make it easier for me to learn, she hit upon the idea of associating each letter of the Hebrew alphabet with a familiar object that had a similar shape (without suspecting that in doing so she was following in the opposite direction the path that led, in the history of writing, from ideograms to alphabetic characters). I still remember that I had persistent difficulty in recognizing the final *tzade*, until she showed me that with its long, delicate stem and the two leaves atop it, it looked very much like a sprig of fresh mint: that immediately – and, as can be seen, permanently – solved my problem. For still more than parsley or coriander, mint was for me the familiar plant par excellence: every morning, it flavored the tea I drank at breakfast, and every Saturday evening, its fragrance accompanied the blessing that marked the end of the Sabbath; and this had led me to plant my own seedling in a little pot, which I watered assiduously.

Thanks to my mother's method, I learned (rather quickly, it seems to me, and with delight) to identify all the consonants, even the ones that – this seemed to me the height of strangeness at the time – had the bad habit of changing form according to where they came in the word (lengthening in the final position). My mother had rapidly found a way to justify this peculiarity by explaining that these consonants were, after all, only 'stretching their legs to rest up when they come to the end of the word.'

The following stage has left me a somewhat less pleasant memory: I had difficulty, at least at first, in grasping the notation of vowels by means of a system of marks and points. My mother had begun by telling me, to encourage me, that if the consonants were the words' body, the vowels were their soul. This seemed to me, so far as I remember, pretty obscure. Moreover, the system appeared pointlessly complicated. I wondered, for example, why there were two different signs for the *a* (the *patah* and the *kametz*), as well as for the *e* (the *segol* and the *tzere*); why, in some cases, two signs were associated with a single consonant. But I did not dare question my mother concerning all these mysteries, and I resigned myself to accepting just as it was everything she was teaching me. All the more because some of these vowels were after all not lacking in charm: I was fond of the *hirek* because it resembled a tiny chickpea, and the *segol* because with its three dots it was like the beginning of a small bunch of grapes.

Thus I was able to begin deciphering a few lines in my old book, the ones that were printed in very large, square letters, and seemed to float, isolated, in the middle of certain pages. This went on for several weeks. And then, one day, I noticed with delighted amazement that I could, with my index finger pressed to the page and sounding out the successive syllables one by one ('Ba-ru-kh a-tta A-do-nai e-lo-he-nu me-lekh ha-o-lam a-sher ki-de-sha-nu be-mi-tse-vo-tav ve-tsi-va-nu'), recognize some of the words, and even sentences, that my father uttered or sang at the important moments of family life (before dinner on Friday evenings, for instance, or before noon meal on Saturdays). This seemed to me virtually miraculous. So words that had up to then seemed to me infinitely far away, because they belonged to the adult world par excellence – the world of my father, the world of prayer – would no longer be out of my reach!

Another memory is associated with this first book. A somewhat later memory, and so deeply imprinted that I can still imagine that I am reliving it. It is late in the afternoon. I am in the kitchen, once again alone with my mother. I have recently learned to decipher words without her help, and I have just finished reading a little bit of the evening prayer. Suddenly, as a result of some movement (a reflex proceeding from fatigue, or perhaps simple clumsiness?), the book slips out of my hands and falls. My mother turns around, sees the book on the floor, and thinks I've thrown it down on purpose. She gets angry, she scolds me, which is quite unlike her. Her reaction makes me understand that, in letting the book fall, I must have committed a serious crime. I therefore accept her reprimands without saying anything and resolve never to do it again. This was, apart from the Sabbath prohibitions, one of the first acts that were for me explicitly linked with the idea of impiety and associated with the word *sin*, or rather – for this was still the period when I gaily mixed Arabic and French – with the Arabic word *haram*, which in our house referred to any kind of violation of religious rules. I had thus learned very early on that if the proper use of a book – handed down from generation to generation as a family secret – could provide access to the most arcane secrets, any carelessness, even if accidental, in this redoubtable domain, threatened to produce in return, for anyone who allowed himself to indulge in it, the most terrible consequences.

This primordial book, solemnly placed on the very threshold of my life as a reader, was before long eclipsed in my veneration by another one. Another one that was still more imposing, by its external appearance (its shape, size, weight – everything about it was singular, exceptional) as well as by the veneration that surrounded it. It was the Sefer Torah, that is, the Book of the Torah, in the ritual form of the great parchment scroll containing the text of the Pentateuch. I discovered it when, at about the age of six, I began regularly to go with my father on Saturday mornings to the synagogue. Every week, during the service, I saw 'the Sefer' (that is what it was called) emerge with great ceremony from the Ark, enveloped in a velvet mantle embroidered with gold letters that seemed to me sumptuous, and crowned with silver ornaments and bells. It was slowly carried through the synagogue, accompanied by chanting; some of the faithful approached it very closely in order to kiss it, while others just touched it with their fingertips as it passed by. Then it was carried up on the dais that occupied the center of the synagogue, where all its ornaments were ceremoniously removed, in order to open it before the audience. Only then did the cantor begin his chanted reading of the text for that day: without the slightest hesitation, he read directly from the parchment, using a thin silver rod in the form of a hand that allowed him to follow the text word by word. The first two or three times I observed this whole spectacle, I was undeniably moved. Later, my father thought it appropriate to add a few bits of information about the very strict rules under which the scribes who copied the sacred text worked: they must not let any error occur, must not make the slightest scrape; otherwise the scroll could not be used. This only increased my emotion.

But a few months later I had still another reason to be deeply moved. This was on the occasion of the festival of the Simhat Torah (the Rejoicing of the Law), which celebrates the end of the annual cycle of the reading of the Pentateuch and its recommencement. Then I saw emerge at the same time, amid the most joyous chants, all the scrolls contained in the Ark (five or six of them). Each was taken by one of the faithful, apparently long ago designated for this honor. Then all the bearers, among whom were the most venerable men in our synagogue (those whose hands I respectfully kissed every Saturday at the end of the service), began to shake, at arms' length, the heavy scrolls caparisoned in velvet. And in the midst of the tinkling of the bells, while the cantor's voice was drowned out by the force of the general chanting, everyone tried to make his sacred scroll twirl as a dancer makes his partner twirl.

Thus for me, from the start, reading and praying have been linked, a lesson that was confirmed when I was old enough to observe the relationships my father entertained with the several dozen volumes that constituted his Hebrew library. Many of them he had inherited from his father Mimoun, who had himself inherited them from still more ancient ancestors, from his own father David or from Yonah his grandfather: there were so few religious books in nineteenth-century Morocco, where there was not a single press, that they were handed down from generation to generation as precious treasures. For the most part, they had been printed in Vienna, Livorno, Kiev, or Vilnius (on the flyleaf of one of them there was even a short handwritten inscription in Hebrew, by which Mimoun records the birth of his son David, 26 Adar 5624 – 24 April 1894). My father kept them in his personal cabinet, the one to which he alone had the key, where he also deposited various objects considered as precious (family documents, including an ancient 'certificate of protection' on which his name was carefully written in black ink, in both French and Arabic, titles to the few bits of property he still owned, old account books covered in black canvas, big envelopes containing an embryonic stamp collection all jumbled together, and a purse full of small gold and silver coins, some round, others square, from the period before the Protectorate).

Aside from the rituals corresponding to the principal Holy Days (which I very quickly learned to recognize, for I sometimes had occasion to use them during my pious period), there were also volumes that long remained mysterious for me. What intrigued me was the incredibly cut up appearance of their pages. Instead of a continuous text, they often contained, around a short central fragment clearly set apart and which I could almost decipher, as many as five or six other separate texts: printed in different characters, in different type bodies (some of them truly minute), they formed unequal masses, blocks, columns, that seemed to overlap each other, imbricated as in a puzzle. Later on, I discovered that these were volumes of the Talmud, with their characteristic arrangement: at the center the Mishnah and the Gemara, surrounded by the cohort of subsequent commentators.

My father, it seemed to me, referred to them only on rare occasions, to find explanations or clarifications regarding some obscure ritual prescription. He was not really a specialist, but like many of his contemporaries, had received a training that permitted him to navigate on the ocean of the Talmud without drowning in it. As for myself, I loved most of all the intimate ceremony with which he surrounded these consultations. First there was the solemn opening of the mysterious cabinet: a good time for me to sneak an indiscreet glimpse of the paternal 'treasures' (whose value I much exaggerated, as I was to discover, a few years later, to my great regret). Then there was the search, slowly conducted, for the right volume. The books were piled up without order in the cabinet, which was too small, and my father carefully examined them one after another, taking advantage of the opportunity to look into the state of their health: some of them still had their original binding but were beginning to show signs of fatigue; others seemed more seriously afflicted, with pages torn by too-hasty handling. The appropriate volume finally having been found, it was still necessary to search out the right page. My father shook his head with an annoyed air until he found it. Then came the deciphering, which was sometimes laborious: the commentators' laconic text could be very obscure. But in general, it all ended with a large smile of contentment, which he accompanied by nodding his head and pursing his lips appreciatively when, the solution having been found, the book-oracle could be put away until the next time it was needed. Then the only thing left to do was to slowly close the treasure cabinet and slip the little black key back into his pocket.

Later still, I came across the book again in every phase of my brief but very intense religious 'career.' In reality, there was no pious event that could get along without the appropriate book(s). Some of them, frequently consulted, remained constantly at hand: the one that contained the ritual for ordinary days, whose pages were worn from constant use; the one for Saturday, more elegant, bearing in its binding and even in its typography – large characters for the Torah, smaller, more rounded ones for the Targum (that is, the Aramaic translation), and others, still smaller, for Rashi's commentary – a reflection of the Sabbath's majesty;

accompanying these two, the little volume of Psalms to which my father devoted, quite regularly, part of his time. The others I saw emerge from my father's cabinet for only a few days each year. These were the rituals for the High Holy Days. Each of them retained, in its external appearance, severe or gay, and occasionally even in traces of drink and food staining some of its pages, a little of the peculiar atmosphere of the celebration to which it was devoted. I quickly grasped the relationship linking Pesach (Passover), Shabuoth (Pentecost), and Sukkoth (the Festival of Tabernacles) when I noticed that the same book was used for all three: it sufficed to change a few words, a few paragraphs, to adapt the prayer for one or the other.

One of these rituals, the one for Yom Kippur, intimidated me: it was used only once a year, and its contents were, in part, very different from those of the others. There were in this volume any number of texts of which I understood virtually nothing. Bristling with strange-sounding words, they seemed to possess an extraordinary solemnity. I discovered a little later that they contained a description, detailed and poetic at the same time, of the service celebrated by the High Priest in the Temple at Jerusalem, and I was particularly sensitive to the double impulse that animated them: nostalgia for ancient splendors marked by the haunting refrain, 'When the ear hears the tale, the soul is filled with sorrow,' but also the hope that a restoration is near at hand. Others, especially those that went with prostration and confession, were a little less inaccessible for me: without grasping the meaning, I was at least capable of perceiving their formal beauty due to the constantly renewed variety of their rhythms and their rhymes.

Finally, there was, in the the paternal cabinet, an object which, because of its resemblance to the Sefer Torah (of which at first I had believed it was merely a reduced copy), awakened my curiosity. It was our old megillah: a little handwritten parchment scroll containing the story of Esther and Mordecai, which was unrolled – very carefully, for it was fragile – only on the evening of Purim, when the story was read in its entirety. It had immediately fascinated me by its archaic appearance, and this fascination grew still stronger when my father assured me, with pride, that to the best of his knowledge, it had been in the family 'for at least four generations.'

Thus the word *book*, which was for me already heavy with resonances, took on an increasing weight. Finally, it even acquired a vital importance in my fantasies. An evolution in which the complex ritual of the two long days of Rosh Hashanah – the most redoubtable days of all, on which the beginning of the religious year was celebrated with austerity – played a not negligible role. For the prospect of hearing the sound of the shofar gave everything that happened on those days a particular emotive charge. Like everyone around me, I waited impatiently for the moment – toward the end of the morning – when the ancient ram's horn was to make its entrance. Its bellowing – four modulated notes, at first sounding slowly, then more and more rapidly, in the unusual silence of the packed synagogue (even our mothers and our sisters, by a special exception, were crowding over the threshold, straining their necks and their ears to participate in the event) – gave me the feeling that I was suddenly, and for a few interminable minutes, on the same level as the world of the patriarchs, the world I was currently discovering through my mother's stories. At the same time, it resounded in my ears like an anguished call for attention, awareness, repentance. It was also in the course of these memorable mornings that, standing in the midst of the chorus of the faithful, I repeatedly uttered the words by means of which we beg God to 'inscribe our names in the Book of Life.' I can still hear this sequence and its intonations. 'Kot-ve-nu be-se-fer-kha-yim': syllable by syllable, in unison, the voices rose up, became almost a cry, then, as if they were exhausted, suddenly crashed and broke in dispersion on the *yod* of the word *hayim* (life). The link was made in an indelible manner, in an atmosphere of sacred trepidation, between the book and the preservation of life, of my life.

Later on, how often I thought about that Book of Life God is supposed to keep, and which He brings up to date at the beginning of each year, when He has decided 'who shall live and who shall die'! At first I tried to imagine it, as concretely as possible. I saw it, rather than in the usual form of a book, as a gigantic parchment scroll unfurled somewhere in the heavens, on which were written, in tiny Hebrew letters that were lost among so many others in long, compact columns, the names of all the members of my family. I shuddered at the idea that other people I knew might have been dropped from the list, and I wondered if God didn't also have, somewhere, a Book of Death, whose contents people preferred not to discuss.

The memory of these moments was so firmly impressed that it has often come back to me. For a long time, I could not look at a list of names, especially the names of Jews, without a certain shiver. A shiver of anger when I came across, in a library, one of those anti-Semitic pamphlets of the thirties that assailed, using endless lists, 'the Jewish invasion.' I could look, to the point of falling into a stupor, at these long series of names in the arbitrary order of the alphabet: a myriad of individuals, whose links with Judaism were usually tenuous, sometimes nil, and whom these pamphlets tried to make appear, by arbitrary juxtaposition, a dense and threatening group. A shiver of rage later on, when, entering with my parents, who were pale with emotion, into the great crypt of Yad Vashem in Jerusalem, I discovered the large plaques of black marble on which are engraved the names of the victims of the genocide. The thought passed through my mind that this was one of the most sinister parts of that Book of Death that had so troubled the first autumns of my pious childhood.

But there was more, fortunately, than this dramatic aspect. The books and pious readings were also linked with far less tense moments. For instance, the evening meetings that were held during the last weeks of the summer, in which I was proud to take part like an adult. It was just after we had moved into the new house. My father was now able to take up again a very old family tradition, which the war had forced him to interrupt. Each year, as the solemn festivals of Rosh Hashanah and Yom Kippur approached, he organized long nocturnal gatherings devoted to extensive readings and prayer. On those evenings, after dinner, there arrived at our house, in little groups of two or three, at least a dozen men in black skullcaps, with salt-and-pepper beards, and wearing gray djellabas. Most of them I did not know; they did not belong to the family, and didn't even speak French. I looked at them curiously: they so closely resembled the people on the antique postcards (in the 'Morocco Illustrated' series) that could still be found in the old part of town, at the newsstand in the Rue Rouamzine, and which represented 'Jewish artisans [tinkers, shoemakers, or carpenters] sitting in their shops'! My father welcomed each of them, exchanging a few words with one or another. Sometimes, a neighbor or relative also joined the group, but a little later in the evening. In order to receive so many people, the back room, which looked out on the garden, had been, the day before, entirely emptied of all its furniture and transformed into an 'Arab living room': on the floor, a woolen carpet from Rabat; arranged in a square around a low table, thick mattresses covered with cushions and pillows. Our guests, having removed their slippers, slowly took their places there (and I with them), exchanged comments I didn't really understand. Then, from the depths of their old leather bags, which they wore bandolier style like the Arab merchants at the cattle market, they took out books, huge wrinkled handkerchiefs, little tin boxes full of snuff, one after the other. When everyone was seated, my father sat down cross-legged beside them. The serious business was about to begin. On the low table was set our biggest copper tray – the one that was usually in the little blue living room – with two teapots and a multitude of multicolored glasses. The boiling hot tea – which for once my father, too busy with his tasks as host, had not made himself – was poured into the glasses with the customary expansive gestures, and the fragrance of the fresh mint immediately filled the room. Our guests drank their tea slowly, in little sips, sometimes making a clicking sound with their tongues. Then, after various blessings that served as a prologue, they all opened their books; and they launched by turns into a long psalmody, which alternated, at more or less regular intervals, with bits recited in chorus by all of them. The snuff boxes were passed around, the last drops of cold tea ('the best part,' they said, with a greedy smile I wouldn't have expected on these faces, which seemed to me rather severe and unattractive) were swallowed, discreet sniffing and sonorous sneezes punctuating everything. And this went on, with a few brief interruptions, until the first rays of dawn. Then, as soon as the morning prayer was said, everyone rose, and the garden was filled with the people who needed to stretch their legs. The tea ceremony began again. But this time, I took part in it. For the tea was accompanied by the piping hot Arab fritters, voluminous and crusty, which were my favorite treat, and the anticipation of which helped keep me half awake.

During this same period, the word *book*, closely linked until then with the multiple manifestations of religious practice, began to take on a quite different meaning, with quite different attractions.

First of all, because of the schoolbooks, and particularly the ones that were then called 'books of readings.' Each fall, during my first years at the elementary school, was an opportunity to discover a new one. As soon as I had it in my hands, I jumped over the opening pages, which were full of grammar and spelling lessons, and rushed on to the final pages, which were reserved for the true 'readings': these were little fictional texts, the first ones I had had a chance to read, and which led me to discover the thrills of an unknown pleasure.

But the real leap happened later, when I began to take an interest in my elder brothers' books. The discovery of these took place in two stages, which have remained linked in my memory with two particular places in the house where we were then living, in the Rue du Dispensaire (the house in which I was born, just across from the hedge of flowering bushes that bordered the courtyard of the school for girls): 'the-closet-with-the-broken-door' and 'the-cellar-with-snakes.' Through them, I was gradually to escape from the gravitational attraction of the paternal sphere – the sphere of strict religious tradition – in order to enter upon a domain that was broader and more open to the world.

When I noticed them for the first time, these marvelous books, they were in the bedroom of my eldest brother, who was at that time the only one who had a whole room to himself in our little house. This bedroom had begun to intrigue me very early on, because it seemed to me that my mother was particularly concerned to keep it clean and orderly. But what in my view distinguished it from the other bedrooms, which were mainly jammed with beds, mattresses, sheets, and blankets, was the presence of a large table made of dark wood and covered with carefully arranged file folders, and especially the large quantity of books that had been placed there. There were neither glassed bookshelves nor volumes bound and gilded, to be sure; more modestly, a cupboard built into the wall, whose door with crude, cloudy glass was cleanly broken off halfway up. In it were deposited over the years, in successive strata, all sorts of books. The bottom shelf was the one in the greatest disorder. It was also the one I knew best: I could reach it without needing to climb up on a chair. From it I picked out the first works I was able to handle freely, smell, dust off, page through, sometimes decipher, and even, without fearing that I was committing a great sin, let fall on the floor. I had invented a game that consisted, on certain mornings, of putting four or five volumes into an old satchel I had found somewhere, and dragging it behind me as I went around the house.

The second stage began by chance, several months later. Below the house's ground floor there was a little room we called the cellar. I never went there: it seemed to me too dark, and I imagined it to be full of snakes and scorpions. However, one day, at the beginning of the great cleaning that each year marked the approach of Passover, my mother ordered me to come with her into the cellar to help her bring up various kitchen utensils she wanted to wash. I grudgingly obeyed. And thus it was that I discovered – instead of the swarm of reptiles which, terrified, I had prepared myself to confront – a bunch of bric-a-brac: old pieces of furniture I didn't know existed, suitcases overflowing with worn-out clothes, lots of bottles (some empty and dusty, others carefully corked and full), as well as various other objects I was incapable of identifying (among which was an ancient film projector with an enormous lens, and – as I was to learn shortly afterward – a number of Max Linder films). But what rapidly drew my attention was the presence, in a corner, of a few cartons full of magazines and books, which turned out to be what are usually called 'children's books.' They were the first of that kind I had seen. From that day on, the cellar ceased to be a forbidden place. I started paying it regular visits, more and more frequent, longer and longer. Every time I came back up with one or two volumes I thought I could understand, though this was not always true.

By what stroke of chance did I begin by discovering an illustrated book entitled *Tales and Legends from the Iliad and the Odyssey?* It was to introduce me to a universe of whose existence I was vaguely aware, but about which I still knew almost nothing, the universe of the 'pagans' and 'idolators.' This was a shock. Everything was so different from what I had learned up until then! I could have (and probably should have) been revolted by this new world, in the name of my vigilant piety. This Zeus whose marvelous interventions I eagerly awaited – wasn't it his statue a wicked 'pagan' king (I even knew his accursed name, Antiochus) had once wanted to put up in the Holy of Holies, in the very heart of Jerusalem? Wasn't it this abominable pretension that had provoked the revolt of the Maccabees, whose victory we commemorate each year in the month of December, with the ceremony of the lights at Hanukkah? Yes, but there it is: instead of feeling the expected revulsion, and through a betrayal I still cannot clearly explain to myself, I allowed myself to be seduced.

From that moment on, I was caught up in an endless spiral. After the Greek narratives, I moved on to the Roman ones. In all logic, I should have rejected with horror the Romans even more than the Greeks, since all I knew about them was that 'their very name made the universe tremble' (a phrase I had heard my mother use several times) and that one of their rulers, Titus (whose name, in the slightly altered form of *Tétos*, was commonly used among us as an insult), had destroyed the Temple. The circumstances, on the contrary, wickedly conspired to bring me closer to them. Thus, during the summer that preceded my entry into the lycée, I had spent three weeks at the seacoast with my sister Marie: thinking about her baccalaureate examination, she had taken along, among other 'vacation reading,' a Latin manual. One day she took it into her head (but later she insisted that in fact the idea was mine, and perhaps she is right) to make an unexpected proposal: to use the long hours normally devoted to the afternoon nap – an (in)activity I never indulged in other than grudgingly – to teach me the rudiments of Latin grammar. It began as a kind of game; I took part in it with increasing pleasure; the manual quickly became our inseparable beach companion. My sister thus got me to swallow, without difficulty, the basics of the declensions and conjugations, as well as a large part of elementary Latin syntax. I was soon able to translate a lot of little texts in which there were sometimes young warriors full of ardor and courage, sometimes noble old men full of proud simplicity. All this durably entrenched, in my life as a child, Roman antiquity, its heroes and its rhetoric.

At first, these new passions had little effect on my religious fervor. That was because I had a sort of antidote. Digging about in the cellar, I had come up with a pamphlet entitled *Sacred History*. There I had had the joy of rediscovering most of the stories my mother told me – in almost the same terms – in the course of our Sabbath conversations: 'Noah's Ark,' 'Abraham and Isaac,' 'Joseph Interpreting Pharaoh's Dreams,' 'Moses before the Burning Bush' . . . having them there before my eyes, black on white and sometimes accompanied by tiny illustrations, whereas up to that point they had existed only through my mother's storytelling, reassured me. I could hurry back to them, in order to 'purify' my mind, when I had spent too much time – and especially, taken too much pleasure – with the heroes and gods of the 'idolators.' I already accepted the coexistence within me (even if it was sometimes with misgivings and at very different levels of belief) worlds that contradicted each other.

With these experiences, a second series of books thus came to take its place in my everyday life. But this one had nothing in common with the first – paternal – series other than the name *books;* and it seemed to me that the fine word *fraternal,* in its double meaning, could rightly be applied to them. There is no point in drawing up the endless list of them here. I cannot, however, forego mentioning at least Jules Verne and Alexandre Dumas, with whom I fell in love just at the moment I was entering secondary school. For months and months, with an enthusiasm that only grew as I made further discoveries, I devoted almost all my leisure time to them. Sometimes even to the detriment of the sacrosanct Saturday afternoon movie. Thursdays, more than Sundays, were particularly favorable to reading. Immediately after lunch, I sat down in the garden with a new volume, a basket full of oranges or tangerines, a couple of packages of cookies; and I did not leave my chair until I had reached the end of the book.

This love I shared with a few friends, which resulted in an intense exchange of volumes among us. We had set up a sort of common depository, which each of us tried to enlarge by skimming all the libraries to which he had access. What excitement when we learned that a new title had appeared and was going to be put into circulation! But what an additional delight when we could rediscover one of our heroes (Joseph Balsamo, Ange Pitou, Bussy d'Amboise) in new adventures! We were all eager to take our turn. And once the book was in our hands, obviously we had to read it very quickly, in order not to keep the next reader waiting.

Thus I had become accustomed to long – very long – nocturnal reading sessions: darkness and silence gave what I was reading an irreplaceable savor. And I could always, in order to justify to my mother these excesses, which she disapproved of, but confronted with which she felt powerless (and she didn't even really know just how bad it was), take shelter, as was my habit, behind illustrious predecessors, impenitent nocturnal readers like myself. In this case, I took my excuse from the best sources, nothing less than the Haggadah for the evening of Passover: it was the episode of the rabbis of Bnai-Berak (I loved their picturesque names, especially that of Rabbi Eleazar ben Azariah and that of Rabbi Tarfon, whose conjugal problems I did not yet know about) who commemorated the flight out of Egypt with such passion that they spent the whole night at it and were surprised to see their disciples arriving to call them to morning prayers. (I took a new interest in this episode later on, when I discovered in it a rather beautiful example of *mise en abyme:* within the text commemorating the flight out of Egypt, the adventure of people commemorating the flight out of Egypt is mentioned, an idea I intended some day to develop at greater length.)

My intimacy with books increased as I grew older, since the pleasure of reading was no longer my sole motivation. I had begun to take a strong interest in other aspects, other faces of the world of books: printing, typography, page design. My initiation into this realm took place when I was about twelve, during one of the weeks in August we spent in Rabat when the heat in Meknès became unbearable. At that time we stayed in the building about which my mother had so often spoken, the one my grandfather Menahem had long ago caused to be built for his children. Two apartments, each occupying a whole floor, still sheltered the oldest members of the family, Aunt Jamila and Uncle David. We stayed, my parents, my little sister and I, with one or the other of them. For me this was like entering a different world. Our stay in Rabat was, from the first minute to the last, an opportunity for an impressive series of discoveries. In these rather shabby apartments, which nonetheless retained some vestiges of their former charm (a terrace with an overhead arbor, a wall phone with a varnished wooden base, deep bathtubs resting on cast-iron legs in the form of lions' paws), I felt at the very heart of our family history. An impression that the personality of my Uncle David reinforced: more than any of my mother's other brothers or sisters, he seemed to belong to the mythical world of the ancestors. I loved his eternal smile full of tender affection, his weary, sweet face, his short white beard (very 'Third Republic,' it reminded me of the one I had seen in a photo of my grandfather). But it was above all his melodious voice, which was also a little hoarse, and his so elegantly refined French that charmed me. That year, he had taken me, thinking it might amuse me, to the print shop he owned a few doors down the street, which was run by one of his sons. He taught me a couple of new technical terms (*lowercase, composition*), showed me the leads and types, and patiently explained the operation of the big presses that, with a clatter that immediately struck me as agreeable, regularly spat out rectangles of paper covered with fresh ink. This plunge into an artisanal world that I knew nothing about pleased me to no end. I returned to the shop as often as I could. In the car that took us, shortly afterward, back to Meknès, I was several times on the point of telling my parents that I wanted to become a printer. As soon as I arrived home, I announced my decision to all my friends who had gathered for the evening stroll along 'the boulevard.'

My needs for books becoming more and more difficult to satisfy, I had to adapt. I first learned to diversify my curiosity, discovering, beyond novels, other kinds of works: dictionaries and elementary encyclopedias, biographies, memoirs. Next I learned to multiply my sources of supply: the school library, books borrowed from my friends, and sometimes trades and purchases as well. But I did not have sufficient funds to patronize the two big bookstores on the avenue (Vielfaure, Solari): the money for my 'weekly expenses' was barely enough to cover my daily *pain au chocolat* – sold by the lycée's concierge during the ten o'clock recess – and my Saturday movie. Thus I limited myself to what I could find among the junk displayed by a few poor wretches who laid out their wares on the ground in a small, crowded square in the old mellah: occasionally there was an old popular edition, with a gaudy cover, of some adventure novel I had long desired. Then, even its bitter ammoniac odor – which in other circumstances would have been an insurmountable obstacle – did not prevent me from diving into it, into the midst of unexplored forests, caverns crawling with snakes, deep gulfs to be crossed, trembling with fear, on a bridge made of vines and shaken by a violent storm, mountains covered with fires at night, and the sound of drums, flutes, and cymbals.

But especially I discovered the pleasures of exploring books that had been collected by other people. Uncles, aunts, cousins, family friends: as soon as I glimpsed the possibility of gaining access to a new lode of books, I neglected no one and even abandoned my proverbial shyness. How many hours, days, sometimes weeks I have spent digging through these collections! They were often disparate, not to say odd; but alphabetical order, with its implacable objectivity, assigned each author his proper place: a few slim volumes of Balzac valiantly filled the gap between the complete works of Amédée Achard and Pierre Benoit, Hugo slipped in just before Jean Jalabert, and one or two Zolas were always pitifully at the end of the line, far behind the abundant production of Maxence Van der Mersche and Max du Veuzit. Since then, I have often wondered what strange and fluctuating criteria had governed these collections. I nevertheless owe them a few moments that I cannot forget.

For instance, those weeks of pure pleasure at the heart of the torrid summer of 1953. This was, politically, one of the most agitated periods I have lived through, since it saw the deposition, and then the exile, of the sultan (who was not yet called Mohammed V, but rather Sidi Mohammed ben Youssef), which was to lead, less then three years later, to the end of the Protectorate. I found myself in Rabat. But this time, I was alone. I was not staying in my grandfather's building, but with my Aunt Sol, who had children about my age. She lived in a European neighborhood – small apartment buildings and pretty villas – in which I liked to walk around. The Hassan tower was close by, and I never got tired of climbing to the top, running all the way, to admire the panorama. I nevertheless avoided spending much time in the middle of the vast field of ruins (dozens and dozens of broken marble columns) that extended from the foot of the tower, the vestiges of an immense and luxurious twelfth-century mosque. As a result of circumstances I don't recall, some friends of my family, who had gone – as was the fashion – to care for their livers by taking the waters in Vichy, had entrusted me with the key to their apartment, which was right in the middle of the city. An apartment that seemed to me the height of refinement, because of its great, arcaded living room, its imitation antique armchairs, its glass showcases full of tiny figures in molten glass; but its principal attraction for me was clearly the library. I had spotted, on my first visit, a treasure I had been dreaming about for months, a complete edition of the *Thousand and One Nights*, whose 'erotic' character (up to that point, I had seen only insipid adaptations for children) had been enthusiastically praised by one of my cousins, who knew more about such things than I did. Such a windfall might not come along again for a long time; I had to take advantage of it. So farewell to the days of picnicking on the beach, sunbathing on the jetty, where the ocean came noisily crashing in on a pile of brown rocks! Farewell to barefoot walks on these rocks, covered with a gluey moss on which I sometimes slipped! Abandoning without regret swimming and games, I left my aunt's apartment as soon as the noon meal was over and headed straight for my providential retreat, where I arrived perspiring. I settled down, with the shutters halfclosed, in the middle of pillows and cushions, on the bed. My only concession to the extremely hot reality outside was the bottle of ice water I kept by my side in order to regularly dampen my forehead. In this way I devoured, day after day, story after story, all the precious volumes, without skipping a single line. And I recall how often I feared, as I read on, arriving at the horrible word *end*, toward which I nevertheless continually hastened.

I loved everything, or almost everything, in these stories: from the rok that fed on human flesh to the four callenders who were the king's sons. For the sake of the beautiful eyes of Queen Scheherazade, of Princess Badrul-Budur, or Princess Camarlazaman (her name, in which is found the Arabic word for the moon, obviously made me think of my mother's first name, Luna), whose adventures I voluptuously shared, I proudly ignored the events that were taking shape a few hundred yards away from me. These events were nonetheless producing a very real historical drama: in a real palace (whose vicinity constituted for me, in other years, the favorite goal of my walks), a real king, bearing like Harun-el-Rashid the fine title of 'commander of the faithful'; real princes (one of whom was to become, three years later, my classmate at the Lycée Louis-le-Grand[1]), accused of conspiring in wicked plots; true pashas, with white djellabas and aquiline profiles, and sounding high and mighty, come down from their mountain at the head of real tribes that were said to be ready for war. All I would have needed to do, on certain days, was to open a window and lean out a bit in order to see marching beneath me,

1. He was obliged to leave one morning in the middle of class, diplomatic relations between France and Morocco having suddenly been broken off after the plane carrying the leaders of the Algerian FLN from Rabat to Tunis had been turned away by the French military.

by the hundreds, Berber horsemen whose appearance should have fascinated me: their robes flying, rifle barrels sticking up above their turbans, they looked as if they had come directly out of an old album of colonial pictures. But I really didn't want to know about all that, in spite of the alarming headlines that dominated the front pages of newspapers like *Le Petit Marocain*, *Maroc-Presse*, or *La Vigie marocaine*. So that when I came out of the cushy retreat where I had remained closed up during the hottest hours of the afternoon, I found each evening, with the same pained surprise, as I hurriedly crossed the city to return to my aunt's apartment, the last vestiges of the disorders that had marked the day, and whose echo I had heard without batting an eye: closed streets, intersections blocked by tanks, and columns of legionnaires on patrol, submachine guns at the ready. I was not truly conscious of the enormous historical mistake that was behind the policy of repression at all costs that was then being unleashed on Moroccan nationalism; my political consciousness was to be awakened only a little later, at the time Mendès-France took office. However, perhaps I would have felt more concerned by the events had I been, already at that time, better informed about the connections that had linked, in the last century, Jacob Ohana, my mother's grandfather, to Sultan Mulay Hassan. But since on those days I had barely emerged from the uninterrupted delights of the Oriental tale, I was not far from seeing in all this agitation, first and above all, an unpardonable breach of good taste.

At the end of that summer, a few members of my family were becoming uneasy: they would have liked to find a way to temper this reading frenzy. My brother Elie, very devoted to athletics, undertook to persuade me of the charms of physical education, and, knowing how highly I already regarded Latin authorities, never failed to slip into his arguments one of his favorite aphorisms: *Mens sana in corpore sano.* Through perseverance, he succeeded in convincing me that I should go with him to the gym that had just opened in the neighborhood. I did so for a few months, for an hour two (or three) times a week. But while I was climbing without conviction the straight rope or the knotted rope, while I was jumping up and down in cadence or endlessly alternating flexions and extensions, under the skeptical eye of the coach, I never really stopped wishing to visit Ali Baba in his treasure cavern, to sail with Sinbad to the edge of the universe, or to await, in the perfumed boudoir of the fair Diane de Monsoreau, the imminent return of her heroic lover, Bussy d'Amboise. I could hardly wait to get back to my world after all these absurd physical contortions. I finally gave up, to the great despair of my brother, who tried in vain to keep me at it. Farewell, biceps, triceps, pectorals, and all the athletic musculature he innocently hoped to endow me with ...

To show my goodwill, I nevertheless had to learn to distribute my moments of leisure in a better way. Hence I had to limit my readings, make choices, no longer avidly attack every printed surface that came my way. I even learned to restrain what had become almost a reflex: the desire to share my literary enthusiasms immediately. A sociologist once said that we read when we have a market where we can place our comments on what we have read. This is probably true. On the condition, however, that we add a complement: there are readers (more numerous than is believed, and that would be a good subject for research) who, not immediately having at their disposal a market for their commentaries, are able to be satisfied with a virtual market. When I think about some of my readings when I was about fifteen, it is clear that they were not intended to provide me with commentaries for the local market. On the contrary, more than once I had to pretend, for reasons of prudence, that I had simply glanced through books I had actually devoured.

My brother, who had not given up his desire to save me, then tried another method, this time with the complicity of my sister Clo. To get me to 'breathe a little,' they started bringing me along, on Sundays, on the car trips they took with their group of friends. Sometimes these were just simple drives through the surrounding countryside: the vineyards at Toulal, the 'Pagnon Farm,' pretentiously renamed 'Blessed Valley,' El Hajeb, clinging to its cliff, on the edge of the Middle Atlas Mountains. On other occasions, there were picnics that took us a little farther into the mountains, toward Azrou and its (magnificent) cedars, Ben Smine, Ifrane, Immouzer, Sefrou, or lake Daïet Aoua (correct spelling not guaranteed). During these grand tours, I was delighted to rediscover the atmosphere of my first Cub Scout outings, when with the whole pack, with our knapsacks on our backs and very proud of the outfits we had laboriously put together (beret, scarf, shirt, and navy blue shorts), we went off to walk, eat, sing, and play somewhere in the countryside, with the intoxicating feeling that we were discovering nature.

This fraternal effort to distract me from reading thus had, to the great satisfaction of its promoters, a complete success. In fact, I got almost as much pleasure from these trips as I did from my books: they offered me the same kind of escape. With their inviting forests, their little brooks with crystalline water, their cool, shady nooks, these landscapes I feasted my eyes on greatly resembled those of France, such as my books had led me to imagine it. And so, as in my books, I wanted to take all the roads, to go to the end of every path, to dip my feet in every little stream of water. And above all, I found it enchanting to look up afterward, in my dictionary, the names of the trees and plants I had discovered: the oaks, ashes, hollies, maples, viburnums, laburnums, and wild grapevines were so many words that entered into my real life, whereas I had thought they were reserved for translating Virgil.

RESOURCES

I want to fit the Ocean into a carafe.
– Gustave Flaubert, quoted in the
Goncourts' *Journal* (11 February 1863)

So I had conceived – in all modesty – the plan of doing for our Moroccan mellahs, and more particularly for the mellah in Meknès, what others had so masterfully done for the ghettos and shtetls of central and eastern Europe. But in a very different literary genre. It was to be a magnificent epic, essentially centered – filial piety required this – on the history of my family. In it, there would be a resurrection of the past so complete and so true, and at the same time so marvelous, that each of the branches, each of the clans that had been constituted over the past three generations, from the old Moorish houses of Meknès, Fez, or Tangier to the terraced apartments in Rabat or Port-Lyautey, and even in the big, opulent villas of Casablanca's residential neighborhoods, would one day be able, proud and deeply moved, to recognize themselves in it, and commune through it. Thus it would also serve (isn't this one of the major functions of the epic?) as a memory and a sign of recognition for the younger generations: no mother – were she attentive to maintaining living ties to her family history – could feel excused from requiring her children to read it. As for the outside observer (at first, the observer I had especially in view), he would have only to look at these pages with sufficient persistence and, as in those old paintings where an open window reveals a whole city with its bell tower, gardens, towers, palaces, public squares, and crenelated walls, he would gradually see emerging, between the lines, an unknown world. This would therefore be one of those novelistic summas into which we enter as if for a long sojourn in a distant land, and where, even amid shoving, harassment, and insults, we move on avidly, from surprise to surprise; one of those books which, boldly mixing laughter with tears and emotion with irony, procures for the reader the pleasure of discovering from the inside, in all its facets, a universe of unsuspected vitality, from which he will depart only with regret, sorry to leave behind, after a period of intense common life, a group of friends.

I told myself – still just as modestly – that such a work, energetic and unusual, would help fill in, through its influence, an unjust lacuna that had too long gaped in world literature, that it would also – and this was not a negligible benefit – let a little fresh air into French literature, which seemed to me, for the past few years, to have smelled a bit musty.

I had already found (this was neither the most difficult nor the least agreeable part of my work) two sentences that seemed to me suitable epigraphs. In their obvious relationship (you would have sworn that one was copied from the other), they sounded a veritable call for writing. I was prepared to believe that they had been expressly conceived for the purpose of dispelling any possible fears on my part. One of them was from Baudelaire: 'Anyone at all, provided that he knows how to amuse us, has the right to talk about himself.' The other from Flaubert: 'Anyone at all, who knows how to write correctly, could make a marvelous book by writing his own memoirs, if he wrote it sincerely, completely.' This double patronage was amply sufficient to reassure me. Wasn't it already a sort of beginning (for this book had already begun long ago in my head)?

It only remained for me to continue, making the best use I could of the material I had at hand.

The 'work' (as I first referred to it, before opting for the names 'family novel,' or 'family epic') would be in the first place drawn from my own memories, which would serve as its foundation. I could not, after all, pretend I didn't know that it was their importunate superabundance that had given rise to my project! And then, I said to myself, taking them as my starting point would be a good way to show my savoir-faire: I would prove my ability to transform the slightest fragments of my personal experience into truths for everyone. But the work would also be based on various complementary bits of information I had been able to glean all through my childhood: either as a result of genuine little investigations that I had conducted with my parents' help while I was at the lycée, or, when I was still younger and dreamed of being invisible, by having deliberately eavesdropped on certain conversations, those 'grown-up conversations' that flowed on at our house like an inexhaustible watercourse, and which I was not supposed to hear, and still less to understand. A large part of this information, which I called, with a slightly pedantic pretentiousness, my 'subjective documentation,' came from my mother. Her narratives had constantly served as my landmarks. It was she who, by her repeated allusions in the course of our long series of conversations, had aroused my curiosity regarding our family history, at the same time that she was giving me a taste for good stories.

This had all begun while we were still living at the house in the Rue du Dispensaire. There was neither a kindergarten nor a nursery school in our neighborhood, and I was not yet old enough for elementary school. So I spent my days observing what was going on around me. I had observed without difficulty that, except for Holy Days, time was divided into two strictly separated periods: the 'week' and the 'Sabbath.' This division governed the whole pattern of everyday life, in our house and in the neighborhood in general: clothes, food, lighting, serving dishes – and many other things besides – directly depended on it. But what was most important for me was that it also governed the rhythm of my relationships with my mother, and even the content of our conversations.

I didn't much like the ordinary days, which were too numerous, and, except for Friday, always too long. They were redeemed in my eyes only if some unforeseen circumstance – a sore throat or a stomachache, for example – disturbed their overly predictable development. Then, any morning could become delicious. How many times, to my great satisfaction, a providential fever, flaring up in the middle of the night, allowed me to slip shivering into my mother's soft, warm bed, and remain there, protected by what remained of her warmth, long after she had gotten up! Apart from these mornings which illness permitted me to save from sameness and boredom, I had in general to show a great deal of patience.

As soon as I awoke, I knew that the day would be a long one. I still had no toys, probably because of the war. I remember, from this time, only an old rocking horse, whose blue paint was beginning to peel off, and on which I could no longer even rock. My main amusement was watching, at midmorning, the garbage cart go by. I heard it coming from a long way off. Driven by a big Arab who repeated at close intervals, in a loud voice, a sort of cry of victory (always the same noisy call in two unequal parts: 'Mou-ou-ou-ou-ou-l-zbel, Mou – ou-ou-ou-ou-l-zbel'), the cart came jolting along on enormous, spoked, wooden wheels that scraped the dry and stony street with a very unattractive creaking. Then I ran to the door. I liked to see the man go by; with his wide-brimmed straw hat, from which hung countless little multicolored ribbons, he seemed to take pleasure in playing the scarecrow. But I especially loved to to watch the heavy gray horse who was pulling, apparently without effort, the cart loaded with rubbish. He knew his mission perfectly and he fulfilled it without needing direction, with the resignation of an ancient sage. He went along with little steps, shaking his head sententiously, stopping of his own accord before the door of each house, sometimes releasing a long stream of urine or a brief cascade of steaming dung, while his master, with a vivacity I admired, seized the garbage cans in his bare hands and, with a single movement, dumped their dripping contents into the back of his cart.

This event over, the day resumed its dreary course. The only thing left for me to do was to cling to my mother's skirts and follow her, in silence, from one room to another, as she did her housekeeping tasks. The latter were innumerable and, despite the help of a maid who took on the bigger jobs, she spent a large part of her energy on this work: the house, too small for us, was not easy to keep up. But no matter how long the day was, my vigilance did not falter, and I awaited the moment when my mother would turn to me. This moment always finally came, toward the middle of the afternoon.

At that hour, there was a moment of calm in the house; my brothers were off at work, my sisters had not yet returned from school, the maid was busy taking out of the oven the bread that had been kneaded that very morning. Everything was already under way for dinner, whose slow and careful preparation (this was just before the invasion of gas ranges and one-minute casseroles) was the main job of the afternoon. Under the big stew pot full of soup, with its poorly fitting lid, the embers in the little coal stove silently glowed, and the odor of coriander, closely allied with that of parsley and boiled beef, began to emerge sweetly in the dimly lit kitchen.

My mother could finally take a breather. She went to find, under the bed in her room, a little square ottoman she had made herself: stuffed with wool, a few coarse, russet tufts of which were coming out of the split seams, and covered in a heavy cotton material with a pattern of enormous red roses and violets on it, in shades long out of fashion. This was her favorite seat (in all seasons, she liked to be close to the floor), where she settled down, sitting cross-legged, her torso very straight and upright. Then I knew that I was going to be able to snuggle up to her, and that the conversation I had been waiting for ever since morning was about to begin.

She welcomed me with a smile, and knew how to make the most effective use of my patience and my good disposition. Sometimes – her pedagogical concern almost never left her – in order to communicate all sorts of new knowledge: it was during these moments that she succeeded, without ever giving the impression that she was asking me to make a special effort, in teaching me to decipher, one after the other, the letters of the Hebrew and French alphabets. Sometimes she had me repeat after her, marking the rhythm with my hands, the inevitable collection of counting rhymes and little songs that form the basis of childhood culture. Some of these belonged to the Arabic tradition, others to the French tradition, still others comically mixed the two. But whatever the language, at first I understood nothing of what I was singing; it took me a long time to perceive that these rhymes and songs were not just more or less magical formulas that merely had to be lightheartedly repeated.

But as the week went on, the daily routine changed. For the time marked by the Sabbath was not limited to Saturday alone; there was also a whole preceding period of preparation, and I knew very well the signs that in our household announced the approach of the sacred day. It normally began Thursday afternoon, with the sudden (but expected) appearance, in front of the door to our house, of an enormous black donkey. He never failed to announce his presence by a few thunderous brays, and I jumped up to meet him. He was loaded with a double basket full of vegetables and greens, brought to us by the farmer who worked a parcel of land that still belonged to our family. The second sign, which came early on Thursday evening, was the arrival of my father. Usually, he brought back from Khemisset, where his grain warehouse was located, a few precious products: in little earthenware jars, glazed on the inside, freshly harvested honey or some specially salted butter, or else one or two pairs of live pigeons, which he held, like chickens, with their heads down; for me this gave his return the character of a little celebration. Then came Friday, a pivotal day, irremediably twofold. Starting in the morning, this was for my mother a time of intensive work – a real race against the clock – as if the promise of Sabbath repose and happiness had to be paid for, in advance, by an exhausting redoubling of activity. Surrounded by a battery of small, glowing stoves, her face lit up by the reflection of the embers over which a multitude of dishes simmered, she seemed to forget the rest of the world and to be thinking only about what was in her pots. That was because everything had to be ready before nightfall, which marked the 'entrance' of the Sabbath. Everything, that is to say, everything needed for at least three large meals, and for a dozen people. . . . Shortly before five o'clock, she cast a last look around the kitchen and gave the maid her final instructions. Then came the privileged moment, the rite of bathing, a preliminary required for the Sabbath as for any other holy day. When my parents, still all wet and warm, started to get dressed, the house had already taken on a new look. My father began the chanted reading of the Song of Songs, which I listened to religiously, so much so that bits of it still sometimes come back to me:

A garden locked
Is my own, my bride,
A fountain locked,
A sealed up spring . . .

I sought, but found him not;
I called, but he did not answer . . .

Next he got ready to go to the synagogue for the evening service (I was still too little to accompany him, as I did later on). My mother, her eyes closed, her open hands pressed to her face, silently said a brief prayer before lighting, as the Sabbath illumination, a small lamp that was to give, all night long, after the extinction of all other fires in the house, a slender, flickering light. She then sat down, relieved, on one of the two rocking chairs that faced each other on the patio, and I could finally go and sit on her knees and listen to her, at least until my father's return.

Here again, pedagogical concern guided her. Borne along by the Sabbath atmosphere – the pleasure in being alive that suddenly seemed to spread to everything in the house – she launched into pious stories. From one week to the next, the great names of the Bible filed past: Abraham-Avinou (Abraham-our-father), whose father, Terah, was an idolator; Yossef-Hatsadik (Joseph-the-just), who was sold by his brothers; Moshe-Rabbenou (Moses-our-master), who saw Hakadosh-barukh-hou (The Holy-Blessed-be-He) face to face on Mt. Sinai; but also David Hamelekh (David-the-King), who was a great warrior and wrote the Psalms; Schlomo Hamelekh (Solomon-the-King), who built Beth Hamikdash (the Temple in Jerusalem); Esther Hamalka (Esther-the-Queen), who, with the help of her Uncle Mordecai, saved the Jews from the massacre planned by the wicked Haman (yimah shemo: may his name be effaced). And especially Samson, poor Samson, who could fight with only the jawbone of an ass for a weapon, but who was incapable of resisting the wiles of the perfidious Delilah; in spite of his death under the ruins of the temple of the Philistines (a moment that I always awaited with the same anguish, the same trembling), I never got tired of hearing his story. The union, so unexpected in my view, of two generally incompatible qualities, physical strength and piety, would long make him (more or less, until I discovered

Hercules, Tarzan, and Superman) my favorite hero. To the point that this was one of the first texts that, spontaneously, I learned by heart as soon as I could read: I recited it from one end to the other to anyone who would listen.

When my father came back from the synagogue, it was already dark. The rest of the family soon arrived, and the ceremonial of the Sabbath dinner could begin: the blessing of the wine in the silver goblet, which was then passed around the table, so that each of us could wet his lips; the blessing of the two big round loaves of bread, from which my father cut the little morsels he dipped in salt and distributed to everyone; and the invariable menu: chicken bouillon with grilled vermicelli; fish with red peppers and chickpeas.

Saturday was altogether different. There was not much for me to look forward to in the morning. In the absence of any housework, which was forbidden on that day, the house seemed sluggish; then the hour of the midday meal approached; and then the meal itself, which mobilized almost all our energies. The afternoon, on the contrary, could be very rich in pleasant moments, because of the visitors, who were almost always unexpected. Some of these visits filled me with joy. They were the ones during which I encountered people who, although they were very near and very alive, seemed to me to have come from another world.

Aunt Rachel (in reality my mother's aunt and the daughter of the legendary Jacob Ohana) was a striking example: tiny and all wrinkled behind her round spectacles, her hair entirely caught up in a sort of black net, she came into the house with tiny steps, wrapped up in her embroidered mantilla, leaning on a little cane with a silver handle; from her past as a notable's daughter she had retained an imperious voice, an impeccable countenance, and merry good humor. But her appearances were irregular and finally abruptly stopped altogether, to my great regret. I learned, long afterward, that she had certainly been among the 'charming and strange little ladies' that had so struck good old Loti during his visit in April 1889; she therefore constituted the last living link with that event – so cherished in the family chronicle – which I would have liked to ask her about.

Another example was my Aunt Zahra, my father's elder sister, imposing and affectionate like a true grandmother. Her visits were more regular, and I watched out for them. For as soon as she arrived, she took out of her ample, puffy black garment a small package for me, which was wrapped in a knotted white kerchief: sometimes half a candied orange, still heavy with the sugar syrup that filled it; sometimes a slice or two of sesame seed cake, tender and crunchy at the same time; sometimes a big handful of grilled, salted almonds. The more familiar I became with her, the more she became for me a living image of the past.

My first surprise had been to see her lodgings: a low house, in one of the streets of the old mellah; in front of the entrance, there was a well, which I was not allowed to approach, but over which I thought I saw a little leather bucket hanging at the end of a rope; next, there was a roofless courtyard surrounded by three big, windowless rooms; in the penumbra of one of these, which smelled a little stuffy, I made out with difficulty, at the back, a low double bed, a wooden chest, and, in the center, various shiny objects – candlesticks, perhaps, like the ones we had at our house – set on a large, three-footed copper tray. I was also surprised by some of my aunt's habits (the most striking: she always had on her person a small box of snuff, from which she took a pinch, holding it to her nostrils and inhaling it with discreet little sniffs) and by her familiarity with a great body of traditions that seemed to me full of mysteries: recipes, gestures, or formulas that were more or less magical and adaptable to the differing circumstances of life. Her knowledge must have been immense in this domain, for my mother – and even the venerable Aunt Rachel – consulted her and considered her an authority. But it was her conjugal history, worthy of that of a famous Roman matron, that for me did the most to mark her image with the majestic seal of the antique.

The arrival of one or another of these visitors (there were others sometimes, but they left less of an impression on me) was for me an event. It allowed me to immediately interrupt my nap (in fact I was only half asleep, and yet . . .) and gave me an excellent pretext for remaining there, sometimes crouched on the carpet at my mother's feet, sometimes (and I liked this even better, because I felt as though I were playing hide-and-seek) concealed behind her big armchair. Motionless and silent, I took in, without their noticing, the fragments of sentences, exclusively in Judeo-Arabic, that came from their mouths. I avidly filled my ears with these remarks, as if someday I were going to have to repeat the enigmatic messages. In reality, I grasped only a tiny part of them, but it sufficed to make me happy. It pleases me today to imagine that it was from those conversations, which often had to do with the memories of 'olden times,' that my mother drew, at least in part, the information that she was later to transmit to me.

When my mother had no visitors, I enjoyed myself nonetheless. I knew that if nothing disturbed us, she would keep me snuggled against her for a long time. And that then we would have again, as on the day before, the blessed intimate conversation. She liked to answer the questions that gradually, as my Judaic knowledge increased, I grew bold enough to ask her. In response to my need to understand, she gave answers that I of course accepted as truths, without noticing that she sometimes resorted, depending on the case, to systems of explanation that were not very compatible: either strict religion, or certain local traditions rooted in magic, or else considerations deriving from the most empirical science. Her answers almost always bore on concrete problems linked with the difficulties of daily religious observance: how the slightest acts in life – eating, drinking, washing one's hands – were to become an occasion for saying a blessing; what actions one could accomplish without violating the repose of the Sabbath; what foods one could eat during Passover. This often led her to recite edifying legends in which Satan sometimes appeared, sometimes the 'evil inclination' (the one that is in each of us, and of which we must always be wary), and sometimes the Angel of Death. But they were always conquered by a providential intervention, that of a few miraculous rabbis (my mother's favorites were Rabbi Meir, Rabbi Eliezer, and especially Rabbi Daoud Boussidan, who was buried very near the outside wall of the old cemetery, and Rabbi Amram Ben Diwan, whose tomb, in the neighborhood of Ouezzane, had become a place of pilgrimage). In spite of their happy endings, these somber stories frightened me. I preferred the sessions in which she explained to me the particularities of the High Holy Days. At first, I remembered only certain details, which I found as exciting as games: the apple dipped in honey, at Rosh Hoshanah, which guaranteed that the year would be sweet; the chickens ritually sacrificed at Yom Kippur, one for each member of the family, which carried off our sins along with them; at Sukkoth, the meals eaten for a week in a hut covered with rushes built in the garden; the candles lighted in our old menorah, and whose number increased by one each evening; the masks cut from sheets of cardboard, and the deafening rattles shaken on the day of Purim; the big copper tray, loaded with various foodstuffs, that spun over our heads on the evening of Pesach, or else, the same evening, the little quantities of water and wine that were poured alternately into a basin as each of the ten plagues of Egypt was named.

Usually, we stopped around five o'clock. This was the time of the 'third meal,' a ceremony to which my father was very attached. For to show clearly that the Sabbath was a day of delights, the ritual prescribed an extra meal. In our house this took the form of a light collation; a few pastries (which my mother had made the day before) accompanying the traditional glass of tea. A sort of religious snack, in short. Needless to say, I had a marked penchant for this judicious commandment: by elevating the consumption of cakes to the level of a religious obligation, it contrasted in an agreeable way with the inexhaustible machinery of Sabbath prohibitions.

But the part I enjoyed most came when my mother consented to leave the realm of religion. Then it was time to explore an entirely different domain, almost entirely Arabic. The infinite domain of Jeha's jokes, which amused me twice over: because they often turned on words or phrases with two meanings, because I was proud that I could understand, and because the hero's apparent naïveté turned out in the end to be a ruse. The domain (which often overlapped the preceding one) of sayings and proverbs, the little, compact tales that served as a constant point of reference in adult conversations. I sometimes had difficulty in grasping the relation between the narrative – reduced to a few striking words – and the moral that it was supposed to illustrate, and which – contrary to what I was later to find in La Fontaine – was never directly expressed. My mother tried to reconstruct for me the implicit line of reasoning that had escaped me; and she laughed almost as much as I did when I finally understood, and still more when I asked her to repeat it all over again.

She liked to tell stories, and could do it for a long time, with the gravity and attention characteristic of a model daughter. Everything she said then took on the appearance of a whispered confidence, a secret revealed to an accomplice. Perhaps that is why this tone has become for me the norm of all kinds of intercourse, and why I have so long put off transmitting its echo to the reader, in the form of a written text.

These sessions became less frequent as my school education advanced. They were even finally broken off: by then I had so many other things to do! During the week, school, lessons, homework, playing with my friends, the neighbors, the cousins. Saturday afternoon (in spite of the Sabbath prohibition), the movies. We went to see, at the end of the forties, almost exclusively American films, which were the usual fare at the Empire theater, on the main avenue of the new city. 'Cowboy stories' and 'gangster stories,' as we called them, were by far our favorites, whereas we tried to avoid 'love stories,' and more generally French films (with the exception of the ones in which Fernandel appeared) or Italian films, which were shown in the other theaters, the Camera, the Regent, or the Riff (which one fine morning became the ABC).

I also discovered, from time to time, new and exciting amusements, such as the one that for several weeks made my heart pound every night: going out in a car. The war was just over, and there were still very few automobiles in the neighborhood. Hence my pride when my eldest brother got one: an old black Chevrolet with rounded lines and a spare tire nestled in its right fender. My brother had hired a chauffeur, Mordecai, to drive it. I immediately took a liking to Mordecai. His cap, his passion for soccer, and his inability to speak properly (for instance, he greeted me with a sonorous 'Comment que ça va?' that always made me giggle) prevented me from considering him a genuine adult. A sort of comradeship had grown up between us, and rituals were quickly established, including that of the evening drive. During the first days after my brother's car entered my life, my excitement was so intense that once I had gotten out of school all I could do was wait for the car to return. Finally, around six, it appeared at the door of the house. My brother got out, and Mordecai took it upon himself to drive it to a garage situated some five hundred yards farther on. Accompanying Mordecai on this expedition, returning afterward on foot, holding his hand and talking with him, had become the main event of my evening. I made extensive preparations in order to draw from these few minutes all the pleasures they carried within them. First I had to decide whether I was going to sit in the front or the back. The front seat was obviously the more attractive, and at first I always chose it. There, I could watch Mordecai manipulating the levers, ask the name of each of the pedals (laughing when I heard him talk about the one he called, with a linguistic logic to which I pay retrospective homage, 'the excelerator'), on the use of each dial, each button on the dashboard. I could even hope that, when we arrived at the garage, he would let me sit in his seat for a moment, so I could turn the steering wheel and turn the headlights on and off. One time, which has remained memorable for me, he let me turn on the ignition and pull very hard on the starter: how delighted and scared I was when the motor suddenly started to purr! The pleasures of the back seat were of another kind: with more room, I could, standing on the seat with my torso exactly framed in the rear window, look alternately right and left, and, like a modest conqueror, wave discreetly to the friends I saw along the way. I also had to decide on the itinerary. Mordecai had to be begged a little, but he sometimes agreed to extend the length of our 'trip' by taking a left turn down the long, steep street that descended past the new cemetery, or by making a large detour to take 'the boulevard,' along which groups of teenagers were beginning to stroll. In any case I knew I would return to the house completely happy and that my happiness would be increased twofold by the voluble account I was going to give my mother. Now it was my turn to teach her a few things!

Thus, although it was a long time before we resumed our sessions, the complicity that arose from those happy moments remained intact. I rediscovered it without difficulty, a few years later, when, having become a student at the lycée, but having remained an unconditional lover of oft-repeated tales, I started to question my mother, more systematically than I had previously been able to do, about our family history. She had more leisure time then, and was more available than in the distant period of my early childhood. Her tasks had begun to grow less burdensome since the eldest children, both brothers and sisters, had married. The painful worries about money that had so tormented her during most of the forties had almost disappeared. The new house, 'her' house, which she had wanted to be vast and luminous, whose construction she had watched over day after day because in it she saw a tangible symbol of the long-desired restoration of the family, left her moments of respite, even encouraged her to relax, without waiting for Saturday to come around again. She finally had moments when she could have said she was happy, had her whole experience of life not taught her to mistrust happiness and taste it only with her lips (this was perhaps also behind her perpetual fear of the 'evil eye').

When the first nice days arrived, when, after the heavy February rains, an already warm sun began to flood the garden, she could not resist the desire to sit in her old rocking chair. I knew that these moments would be the most propitious for our conversations.

She never shied away from them, and in spite of her fatigue (which was also beginning to show, but which at that time I was not yet able to see – as I was to learn to do much later – in the sudden darkening of her eyes, or, in her very last years, in the gradual weakening of her voice), never needed much urging. All that was required, as before, was a question, or sometimes a casual remark that showed – involuntarily – my ignorance regarding some point that seemed to her important: she was immediately ready to start a long story, to follow one anecdote with another and another.

She was particularly fond of certain important moments in her childhood. For her, they constituted a sort of precious base: in fact the foundation, the anchoring point of her memory as a whole. She recounted them to me many, many times. As if she had necessarily to begin there in order to feel sure of herself and justified in her role as witness. Moreover, she had told these stories so often that they also served, it seemed to me, as a sort of test run: through these preliminaries requiring little effort, she gave herself the time to get up to speed internally, and to be able to go on each occasion, in answering my questions, a little farther in exploring her past. How much she cherished these stories I was was not to rediscover until later. She was then far past seventy, and her eyesight was beginning to bother her; fearing that her memory would also betray her (a dread that turned out to be unjustified: until her dying day, her memory remained completely intact), she resolved to put a few of these stories into writing. And so it was that, courageously, evening after evening, while my father read his countless newspapers or listened to the successive news bulletins he could get on his big black transistor radio (he was a fervent fan of 'continuous news' before it became fashionable), she succeeded, over five or six weeks, in filling, in a fragile and assiduous hand (sometimes omitting commas or accent marks), almost all the pages of a small school notebook. She wrote this title in capital letters on the first page: DISTANT MEMORIES, and gave it to me ('It might be useful to you some day, who knows?') with a mixture of pride and shyness.

She always liked to mention first the great moments she had witnessed. March 1905, for example. She was then not quite five years old. Her parents, Menahem and Esther, had just arrived in Tangier, having traveled by sea from Rabat. She was at their side on a very small boat being rowed toward the port. It was from that vantage point that she was able to observe an extraordinary event: the arrival of the German emperor, Wilhelm II, off Tangier. The meaning of this visit, within the framework of the colonial rivalries in which France and Germany were then involved, had of course totally escaped her. But on this exceptional day, the panicky agitation of a multitude of small boats, canoes, and felucas between the shore and the imposing imperial vessel had permanently marked her, imprinting on her memory a kaleidoscope of images she found it difficult to describe with precision.

Other events gave rise to more detailed accounts, such as the passage, in May 1910, of Halley's comet. My mother described, in short sentences, all the stages of this incredible adventure. She was able to reconstitute the fear that had struck the entire population several days before the comet appeared. Everyone was convinced that the end of the world was imminent: some, being fatalists, barricaded themselves in their houses for a final feast; others, less resigned but just as powerless, no longer counted on anything but their prayers; most, including children, spent their nights on the broad, flat terraces of their houses, their eyes fixed on the sky, looking for the giant ball of fire that was supposed to come and burn everything up (it was expected on the night of the eighteenth). The most curious rumors circulated. It was said that in Europe dozens of people had already chosen to commit suicide before the catastrophe occurred. My mother herself, affected by the general agitation, had decided to indulge in a final pleasure before she died. She got together all the pocket money that remained to her, a few battered, bent, square coins, and hurried to the market to buy a dozen eggs: she simply wanted to make herself an enormous omelette, and to savor it while she waited for the final explosion. But when she had made her purchase, she had such a hard time, in the hurly-burly of streets even more crowded than usual, getting home with her fragile burden, hastily wrapped in a poorly knotted kerchief, that on the way all her eggs broke. She was thus forced to prepare herself to see the earth catch fire and disappear without even having been able to realize her dream – modest enough – of having an omelette.

She then went on, with more or less enthusiasm depending on the day, to a description of her early marriage, and this was for her no longer just a story. I had the impression that, when she had arrived at this point – which was so important – in her personal history, she could not keep from reliving, as if in the present, all its crucial turning points, and I saw in her face, through expressive mimicking, each of the reactions of a young girl caught up by events. Her amused surprise when one afternoon, coming home from school, she found her father's big house jammed with people, baggage, packages of all kinds, and full of an animation incommensurate with what normally went on there: Uncle Mimoun and his family had just arrived, with the caravan and armed escort that had accompanied them on their long trip from Meknès to Rabat. Her incredulity when she told the reason for this move and the sudden agitation it provoked, namely her imminent marriage to her cousin David, in fulfillment of a promise Menahem had long ago made to Mimoun. Her vexation at a decision she was not expecting so soon and against which she had no recourse. She believed she was witnessing the sudden end of her childhood, at the very moment when she was taking the most pleasure in it: not yet twelve years old, she was going to have to give up school, along with the games and the whole new, attractive world she had found there. 'Fortunately,' she added, correcting herself with a little smile (intended to reassure me, or to reassure herself?), 'the break was not so abrupt.' As was customary in these early marriages, after a long series of parties and traditional nuptial rites (which went on over several weeks and whose every detail remained in her memory), she in fact still remained a long time with her parents and her young cousin, who was more a playmate than a real husband. And if, having become a 'lady,' she had in fact to give up going to school, she did not for all that stop learning. Her father had her given lessons, and she was able to continue, with tutors, to study the two languages she had immediately become passionate about: French and Spanish (she added, laughing, that she had never been able to get anywhere with English, which she found 'unpronounceable').

She excelled in portraiture. Admiring and moved when she described a few familiar persons who had influenced her when she was very little: the young lady from Spain (the head of a tiny private school, where she taught elementary Spanish to a few still unrefined Jewish girls, at the same time initiating them into European good manners), who had taken a liking to her and treated her like her own daughter; or Monsieur Conquy, the admirable teacher, who had become a family friend, and from whom she learned French spelling and grammar (more than half a century later, she was still capable of repeating verbatim his lessons on the agreement of past participles!). Sardonic with other people, whom she was able to dispatch quickly: a way of behaving, something said, and the poor man or woman was vividly sketched. For instance, to take only the examples that made me laugh most (because I easily recognized the models of these mocking portraits), there was the 'enlightened man,' so concerned about giving his daughters a modern education that he forbade his wife to say anything to them in Arabic; the 'discriminating man,' who pushed affectation so far that he brought along his own bottles of beer, cooled to the right temperature, when he went visiting; the 'sensitive man,' who retaliated violently when he received the slightest pinprick and who did not hesitate to punish with a yearlong pout (it ended only on Yom Kippur, at the time when all offenses are ritually erased) a simple – unfortunate – lapse on the part of his brother-in-law; the 'parvenu,' with shaky French, who told his beloved, by way of proposing marriage, that he wanted to 'fondre un nouveau foyer'[1] with her and was refused for this reason; the 'scatterbrained woman,' so inept with sentences that she used only exclamations, punctuated by bursts of laughter as sonorous as they were superfluous.

But what she loved most was to talk about a still more distant past, concerning the lineage of her parents, Menahem and Esther. She was very attached to this precious set of memories, and the development of her attitude with regard to them had been significant: the more things changed around her, the more she clung to these recollections. They had moreover helped her endure the difficult conditions under which, in certain periods, she had been forced to live. She therefore preserved them with a pride that it did not occur to her to conceal. All the more because she knew that no one else possessed them, since she alone, spontaneously appointing herself as the guardian of the family memory, had had the idea of collecting them directly from her father (and from a few other people of the older generation, such as Aunt Rachel). Thus she had the intoxicating feeling of transmitting to me, at least on certain precise points, truths that she alone had saved from oblivion: 'genuine historical documents,' as she liked to say.

She sometimes hesitated, or even erred, concerning details:

1. The unfortunate suitor confuses *fondre* (melt) with *fonder* (establish). – Trans.

the date of a marriage or a birth, the name of the father of a second cousin I couldn't place on the family tree – which was still pretty short – that I had begun to sketch out, the age of an old aunt. My father then intervened in these discussions, which gave them an unaccustomed liveliness. Debates about age, the most frequent, could even become bitter: inevitably, when she mentioned a marriage, and especially a remarriage, my mother had a tendency to make the husband older, as if to exaggerate the difference in age separating him from his bride; on the contrary, when she mentioned a death, she spontaneously made the deceased younger, in order to stress the cruelty of a death that was always premature. My father chimed in by providing, with a somewhat acid brevity (for his view of the events and the people was not necessarily equally benevolent), more precise information. And she went right on, as merrily as ever. Which pleased me greatly.

I took advantage of her good disposition to get her to explain, and to repeat again and again, if necessary, episodes I had not followed very well, details I had forgotten. For from the outset, by a sort of tacit convention, I abstained from taking any notes while I was listening to her: that would have risked breaking the rhythm of our 'conversations,' making them seem less natural. And my first concern was to let her stories develop as freely as possible.

This abundant 'subjective documentation' was, in my mind, only part of the necessary material. My mother's memory, even with the occasional supplement of my father's recollections, was not sufficient for all purposes: many facets, many complexities, many mechanisms escaped them both, my mother as much as my father. Of the society in which they had lived, they could not, of course, have a complete view, or even an orderly one. And besides, nothing guaranteed that I had asked the right questions. It seemed to me that countless small enigmas remained unresolved.

Therefore I felt the need to collect – as a complement or counterpoint – an 'objective documentation' of at least equal abundance. In this resided, in my view, the originality of the enterprise and its (possible) interest. The family chronicle, which could always be suspected of being too indulgent, too ready to yield to sympathy and foolishness, would not have the last word. It would be accompanied, and corrected if necessary, by genuine scholarly research: an investigation that would be historical, sociological, linguistic, and even ethnographic, ethnological, or anthropological (at that period I did not distinguish among these last three terms very clearly, and that hardly bothered me at all) . . . in sum, my curiosity would have no limits: nothing that had to do with the human sciences – which were undergoing in those years, around the Rue d'Ulm, a sort of influential renaissance (Bourdieu had just begun a seminar that Althusser had not hesitated to present as marking 'year one of sociology') – would be alien to my project. Moroccan Judaism would be put through the sieve of all the disciplines. Purified by this contact, having finally become an object of knowledge and not merely a pretext for nostalgia, it would recover some of its forgotten nobility.

I had little idea, at this time, of the effort that such an enterprise presupposed. Although none of the indispensable tools – neither accessible archival materials nor repertories of sources, bibliographies, or reference works – existed, I hoped to be able to master my subject quickly, and all by myself, innocently counting on reading that I thought was very extensive. For I had, long before the project had taken form in my mind, begun to accumulate these 'objective' documents. Every text that mentioned, even briefly, the Jews of Meknès (Mekinez or Mequinez in the most ancient texts), or more generally the Jews of Morocco, before or after the establishment of the Protectorate, but especially during the key period for my family, the end of the last century, was suitable for my purpose. Thus I had begun to read more widely on Morocco's past with a zeal just like the zeal I had displayed, a few years earlier, in tracking down books about Paris.

I had been able to bring in a first harvest: articles in old encyclopedias, like the ones in the *Larousse du XIXme siècle;* private notebooks, such as Delacroix's diary, in which, during the months corresponding to the painter's visit to Morocco in 1832, Meknès was often mentioned, and I even had had the pleasure of finding an allusion to a person by the name of Ben Abou (who, I discovered later with a certain disappointment, was unlikely to be among my direct ancestors, since he was in fact a Muslim, and more precisely a chief, Mohammed Ben Abou Ben Abdelmalek, commander of Sultan Mulay Abderrahman's cavalry in Tangier); travel books, like Loti's *Au Maroc,* which had become a family classic because of his account of the visit he paid Jacob Ohana, our ancestor, whom he did not, however, name; tourist guides or journalistic articles, which were more concerned with exoticism than with sociological analysis; amateur ethnological investigations into various aspects of Jewish life.

It was clear that I was going to find myself faced by a whole collection of data of very diverse origins and natures, which at the end of my labors I would have to bring together in a single text. And, of course, I still had no idea how to proceed. I decided, to get a more precise view, to make a preliminary inventory of all the material I would be using. I quickly recognized that it could be rearranged under three broad rubrics, which I immediately adorned with peremptory titles:

— 'Ancient Histories' would include all the narratives anterior to my parents' generation;

- 'The Family Circle' would concern everyone (parents, brothers and sisters, and also a few uncles or cousins) associated with my childhood; and

- 'The Weight of Rites' would provide a portrait of the community that had framed the family saga and that was marked by the constraints imposed on it, in all aspects of its life, by its fidelity to Judaism.

But these rubrics could in no way constitute, in my view, the parts of the future work, which would then have been no more than an indigestible rhapsody. I wished, on the contrary, by judiciously mixing ingredients taken from each of them, to blend them as completely as possible.

I wanted something that would stand up to time, to wear and tear, to fashions. Only the novel, it seemed to me, had the required titles of nobility to carry out the mission my future book had been given. Only the novel was sufficiently supple to adapt to what I wanted to do, which turned around the idea of imbrication. One of my oldest dreams had been a book in which several series of texts, different from each other and yet related, would be juxtaposed, or rather interlaced. Finally – and this was not the least important reason – the taste for novelistic romance had inhabited me for such a long time, favored by a childhood devoted to reading, to dreams, to nostalgia, that I could not, without offending against decency, be unfaithful to it in a matter that was connected, at least in part, with this childhood.

MODELS

*The writer is a public experimenter:
he alters anything he does over; obstinate
and unfaithful, he knows only one art,
that of theme and variations.*
– Roland Barthes, *Critical Essays*

Now it remained only to get started.

The problem was that I was virtually without experience. I knew very little, except by hearsay, about what was going on among theoreticians of so-called avant-garde literature. Nothing had prepared me for writing a novel. Especially not the academic works I had composed up to that point: hackwork more likely to be, for the execution of my project, a handicap. In fact, I had to reach far back into my memories to find a few traces of my old passion for literary fiction.

It was sometime during my adolescence that, like everybody, I made my first attempts in this genre. The most serious I had not carried out alone, but in collaboration. Writing in tandem already seemed to me, as it does today, easier. I still sometimes – quite often, actually – think my literary production would have been greater – in volume(s) – had I been able, at certain critical moments, to share with someone else the cares and pleasures of writing. And one of my regrets, which grows from year to year, remains my failure to complete the various projects (especially *Presbytère et prolétaires, L'Histoire universelle,* and *Le Roman du XIXme siècle* [*Presbytery and proletarians, Universal history,* and *The novel of the nineteenth century*]) conceived during the sixties with a friend who died too soon.

The boy who was, during my adolescent experiments (and virtually since infancy) my closest friend – all the closer because we were also cousins, neighbors, and schoolmates (so close that, as one of our teachers put it, 'to distinguish between the two, you had to get to the third letter of their first names') – shared with me (or perhaps it was I who shared with him) a fascination with literature. Equally insatiable readers, we had finally succumbed, at around fifteen, to the desire to 'go over to the other side' (the formula was ours). And one fine day, under the watchful, half-curious, half-concerned eyes of our respective families, we had begun to write. I remember above all the only two projects we managed to actually begin. The first was none other than the inevitable adolescent novel about the awakening of sensuality (we did not yet, in those distant times, dare to call sexuality by its name). The second was the no less inevitable schoolboy farce, which had the particularity of being written in Alexandrine verse (intentionally bad), on the joyful amusements of school life: the rhyming dictionary was our principal source of inspiration. This went on for a few months: lots of palaver punctuated by a little squabbling and enormous bursts of mad laughter (shared writing, I can testify, bears mad laughter within it as a cloud bears the thunderstorm). After which, we had to admit that even when we combined our talents – which we discovered, in practice, to be very dissimilar – we were definitely not Radiguet, nor Jarry.

I had also started to compose a tragedy, which I intended to be Racinian. But I had to set about it alone: my cousin, who at that time dreamed only of writing a Shakespearean drama, found Racine old-fashioned. I therefore labored, in the greatest secrecy, over the pages, which were annotated with a distressing parsimony, of an old edition of *Selections from Livy* (it had belonged to my elder brother, who had scribbled in pencil, in the margins, the translation of a few difficult passages) in order to draw up a plan for a very moving 'Death of Hannibal.' The subject, which I had set myself after long reflection, was defined (and these are the precise words) this way: 'Hannibal defeated, abandoned by his own people, is pursued even in exile by the Romans' tenacious rancor; resolved to kill himself, he secretly prepares his posthumous revenge.' It seemed to me suitable for ample historical and moral developments: the undeserved defeat after the glory of his victories, the betrayal of his compatriots, exile, the desire for vengeance, the decision to commit suicide – what could be more dramatic? At the same time, it also appeared to contain enough *majestic sadness* to delight the most fanatical Racinians. I therefore drafted a detailed outline, act by act, scene by scene, on the exact model of those then found in the learned prefaces in the *Larousse Classics*, of which I had, thanks again to my brother's legacy, a copious assortment. Unfortunately, I lost this outline, along with most of my adolescent notes and papers, during a move (the very day I moved into my room in the Rue d'Ulm). But I still remember what I intended to put in the final stanzas, the most beautiful part of my tragedy. Paraphrasing fairly cleverly Camille's famous lines in Corneille's *Horace*, I had my hero prophesy, with his dying words, 'of the Roman empire the inevitable fall.'

This verse was to have been the last in the play, which – significantly (I already liked this kind of wink) – would end on the noble word 'fall' (*chute*). My intention was to show, with all the desired discretion, my nascent political consciousness: I had just discovered, thanks to Mendès-France, the condemnation of colonialism. Of course, my play was never completed. I believe I did not even get beyond the twenty-ninth (or the thirty-ninth) alexandrine. I recently found an old file card (dating apparently from the period when I was writing my thesis) on which I had one day decided to copy out (with what obscure use in view?) the very first of these verses. They were, if I am not mistaken, spoken by the eunuch (why he had to be a eunuch, I no longer know; perhaps only for local color) Artaxas, the confidant of Prusias, the king who had given Hannibal refuge, and who was soon to betray him. Here they are:

Oui, de tous vos exploits je connais le récit
Et votre nom, seigneur, vous précéda ici.
Depuis que de Scipion la vindicte barbare
Vous a de votre ville expulsé sans fanfare,
Notre peuple a loué votre comportement,
Espérant voir bientôt la fin de vos tourments.
Car le destin cruel dont vous fûtes victime
Ne vous a point ôté vos droits à notre estime.
Je puis vous l'assurer: en dépit des Romains,
Vous trouverez chez nous l'accueil le plus humain.
Le valeureux Prusias a concu pour Carthage
Une amitié profonde et que chacun partage.
Vivez ici sans crainte . . .[1]

[I've heard the tale of all your exploits,
And your name, my lord, has preceded you.
Ever since Scipio the vindictive barbarian
Expelled you without fanfare from your city,
Our people have praised your conduct,
Hoping soon to see the end of your torments.
For the cruel fate of which you were the victim
Has not deprived you of your rights to our esteem.
I can assure you of this: in spite of the Romans,
You shall find among us a humane refuge.
Valiant Prusias has conceived for Carthage
A deep friendship that is shared by all.
Abide in this place without fear . . .]

1. One doesn't have to be a learned scholar to perceive that my knowledge of prosody left much to be desired: hiatus, padding, unacceptable rhymes abound in this sample. It is true that our teachers, whatever eminent qualities they may have possessed in other regards, gave these issues very little attention.

What strikes me today, apart from the conventional, clumsy, and indecisive character of all this bric-a-brac, is the absence of Jewish and Moroccan themes. As if these concerns, which were going to become so strong a few years later, didn't exist, or at least had not yet succeeded in impressing themselves on my mind. I believe they had all the same filtered in to some degree, but in a disguised form, and remained imperceptible for me. Thus, the choice of Hannibal as my hero (a Carthaginian, that is, a Semite, and moreover an exile, unjustly persecuted by an omnipresent enemy) and the choice of the desire for vengeance as a 'tragic passion' were not without significance. However, for a long time, I refused to see in this any more than a testimony to my precocious interest in those who had dared to resist Rome.

Nothing came of these first attempts and I had written, since then, almost not at all. If my family epic was important to me, I had an urgent need to fill in this gap in my training. What could I do besides resort to imitation, basing my work on models? This was the way I had always proceeded when I didn't know what else to do.

In fact, this had already begun, in my earliest childhood, with aggravating questions of language. It is true that the situation in which I was immersed had something intriguing about it. It was characterized by a mixture of idioms (French, Arabic, Hebrew) and accents (the way of pronouncing the *é* – always closed – and the *r* – rolled in the Burgundian manner or uvular in the Parisian manner – played a central role in this) which required, to achieve proper mastery, constant vigilance. Everything came down, it now seems to me, to a problem of proportions. A greater or lesser measure of Arabic, or rather of Judeo-Arabic, determined a rather subtle hierarchy among the different levels of language.

Thus in our house, at that time, everyday language already rested on a broad basis in French; but a few somewhat specialized sectors, that of the kitchen in particular, remained mysteriously under the rule of Judeo-Arabic (for example, I discovered only later, when I went to the lycée, words like *sésame, cédrat, jujube, coriandre,* or *fenugrec*,[2] whereas their equivalents had been known to me forever). Still, this was not entirely common Judeo-Arabic: it was rather a family variant, whose particularities became apparent to me only as the years went by. I had at first been aware of the presence of a large contingent of Spanish words or locutions I did not find in the vocabulary of my friends, such as the expression *fueras del mal*, which it took me a long time to decode: the formula, intended to preserve from evil the person whom one is about to name, ritually preceded, in my parents' speech, the first names of my elder brothers, and was sometimes even substituted for them; but by being used in this way, it had been deformed to the point of becoming unrecognizable; and so, for several of our maids, who thought it was a second given name – without knowing exactly whose it was – this became something like *Bourazmann*. Later on, when I was able to make broader comparisons, I was struck by a second characteristic, the extraordinary abundance of diminutives in our language (with the result that, when I had to study Ronsard's poem 'Amelette vaguelette ronsardelette,' I was right at home). My mother's influence played a large role in this. In her mouth, almost no substantive escaped this softening treatment (the transmutation into a hypocoristic); as if, pushing to the extreme her desire to attenuate the rigors of the external world for us, she had tried to round off the corners of the words, to erase even the asperities of language. This familiar language, particularly rich in affectionate expressions, was not easily exportable, for fear of ridicule, beyond the family circle. For me, it was in any

2. Sesame, citron, jujube, coriander, fenugreek.

case very different from the language of the street (that of the merchants, of games and conversations with pals), where French occupied a smaller place and might sometimes – rarely – even be absent, and where Judeo-Arabic took a more usual form. As for the language of the elementary school, and still more that of the lycée, an effort was made to limit it almost exclusively to French, and what is more, to a highly refined French.

So that if I wanted to avoid seeming by turns ridiculous, ignorant, or pretentious, I had to be careful, with each new category of interlocutors, to inflect my way of speaking in the proper manner. An amusing intellectual gymnastics that was like a veritable game: it could even become a source of subtle satisfactions, like the feeling of superiority it gave me with respect to those who, reduced to the monotonous manipulation of a single idiom, were ignorant of the finer points of my linguistic pyramid. But a gymnastics that was in the long run harmful: very early on, it accustomed me to modeling my speech on that of others.

This quest for models, which I am still today not far from seeing as one my chief weaknesses, had also been my obsession in many other domains. Is that because in our house, everyday life was subjected to so many rites and rules that seemed to me obscure or arbitrary? The fact is that I lived in fear of making a mistake, of doing the wrong thing. But above all I was afraid that by adopting a nonconforming attitude I would end up disappointing my family, by allowing them to adopt an image of me that did not correspond to the inner feeling of myself that I was beginning to have. Therefore I avoided, as much as I could, any sort of idiosyncrasy. On the contrary, things seemed to me much more reassuring when I could follow a path blazed by a few predecessors.

I had begun very early to seek out predecessors, and first of all among those close to me. The conditions, once again, promoted this. Around me, there was no lack of elders. A first circle: brothers and sisters who were already adults, different in their characters, their tastes, and their occupations. If I extended the field to the family in the broad sense, in which the diversity of types and conditions was even greater, I had at hand a veritable embryonic society, with its contrasts and its hierarchies. I had only to draw on it.

Early on, I had been obliged to grasp the necessity of dividing up the tasks. Thus there took shape in my mind, at around eight years of age, a complex configuration in which each of my family members, spontaneously idealized, was identified by one or two traits, one or two qualities, the very ones I hoped to borrow. My father, a man of prayers, surrounded by an additional mystery given him by his weekly absences (he left the house on Sunday morning, with his everlasting little brown valise in his hand, and didn't return until Thursday evening), was above all piety; my brother Albert, who was already taking seriously his role of eldest son and beginning to succeed as a businessman, was generosity; my brother Elie, whom I served as a messenger in his exchange of letters with his fiancée, was seduction; my sister Clo, who kept a close watch on my schoolwork, was knowledge; my brother Gabriel, who was studying in Paris and sent me letters and postcards (the first mail I ever received), was the prestige, refinement, and delicacy connected with Parisian life. My other sisters, Marie, Anne, and Esther, were too close to me in age, still too involved in childhood or adolescence for me to be able to give them a role in this cenacle, which served as the first food for my nascent mimetic bulimia.

A little later there appeared on my horizon, in successive waves, new personages, who emerged from a family circle that was beginning to expand. I tried, every time I found a good reason for doing so, to assign them a place in my ideal arrangement.

But pulled in too many different directions, my admiration occasionally fluctuated. Sometimes, eager to have courageous captains, fearless knights without reproach, I let my admiration fall on those of my cousins who had fought in the war in Europe; without knowing anything about their possible exploits, I had on my own authority promoted them to the rank of heroes, and they henceforth incarnated the chivalric bravery I had known up to that point only from my history book. Sometimes, dreaming of vast territories, of distant expeditions (and this was the time when the image of a port with boats, jetties, and cranes, or even just the sound of the word 'steamship,' was enough to move me to tears), I turned toward my mother's brothers, in whom I saw genuine adventurers, who had courageously set out to conquer distant lands. Thus I fantasized, when I was nine years old, about my two uncles who had gone, in the years before the war, to seek their fortunes in America. I discovered only later on what their mission had really been. Having been made responsible for the Moroccan pavilion at the 1936 World's Fair in Chicago, they had had the idea – a smart one, after all – of setting up a vast 'Arabic Exposition': fine mosaics and carved wood, thick woolen carpets from Rabat and velvet cushions, a set of samovars in hammered silver, mint tea and almond pastries. But neither the busy bankers from New York, nor the puritan intellectuals from Boston, nor the rustic farmers from the Midwest were really sensitive to the incomparable aroma of Meknès mint, to the delicate exoticism of gazelle's horns, stuffed dates, bigarades, or candied citrons. The American adventure turned out to be a failure.

When I was about thirteen, other problems began to arise for me, which the devices of imitation no longer sufficed to resolve. I had to go far beyond the confines of the family and seek answers elsewhere. At once, I turned to the Jewish tradition. What heroes could it offer to help me understand myself? To be sure, neither the patriarchs, the kings, the prophets, nor any of the great figures of legend and history that my mother's stories had made known to me. The latter, although regularly mentioned in the prayers on Holy Days, now played for me only the role of mute walk-ons; they seemed too remote from my adolescent preoccupations. Fortunately, I had long before discovered many other paths to explore, and it was in a less faraway literature that I sought more accessible models.

This began badly. I had no difficulty in finding (for they were everywhere; these books had apparently enjoyed such success among the French in Morocco that anyone who sold old things had them) a few volumes with seductive titles: *When Israel Is King, The Rose of Sharon, Jerusalem, A Brief History of the Jews*. I am not sure that they have much to say to a reader today, and that does not distress me. For their contents, immediately devoured, at first astonished me, and then, in the most purely physical sense of the word, disgusted me. I was encountering for the first time, in the cunning writing of the Tharaud brothers, the systematic malevolence, the tendentious travesty, the haughty snickering that I subsequently discovered was only the mildest form of a literary anti-Semitism that was to provide me, a little later on, with more violent poisons. What most dismayed me in these spiteful volumes was that the lovely French language – for which I had begun to have a genuine devotion – could, without remorse, be put in the service of such vile goals.

Having emerged from these miasmal swamps, I tried to conduct my investigations more carefully. In order to avoid any risk of disappointment, I set about looking for Jewish authors talking about Jewish heroes. But where was I to find them? In the neighborhood, the only 'public library' – a very grand expression for a very humble reality – was that of the alumni association at the Alliance Israélite school. The 'association,' with its little bar, its ping-pong table, its chessboards, and its books, fulfilled a twofold function: it was a place where everyone could find relaxation and amusement, but it was also, on occasion, a center for debates among a handful of adolescents eager for knowledge. I explored, devoting for several weeks my Thursdays to this task, the two or three hundred bound volumes that were kept in a cabinet with double glass doors. My first discovery was Edmond Fleg. A veritable oasis. In the turmoil in which I then found myself, I couldn't resist a title like *Why I Am a Jew*. This was for a time my bedside book, even if the answers it gave did not really correspond, in the end, to the questions my situation led me to ask.

The same exploration allowed me subsequently to discover, thanks to the stories of Sholem Aleichem and Isaac Leib Peretz, the existence of the Yiddish world, its literature, and some of its curious heroes. I will not soon forget my first encounter with Toby the milkman or with the character who was at once my favorite, and who remained my favorite for a long time, Bontché the Silent. But the joy of this discovery didn't last long. For what I was looking for was not a literary pleasure (which many other things I was reading at the same time gave me in abundance), it was models with whom I could identify. Now, in these authors, I recognized almost nothing of the Judaism that was familiar to me. The characters in their tales had strange names, practiced strange trades, said strange things. In their mouths, the most everyday blessings took on strange sonorities, and even the most common Hebrew words became almost unrecognizable. While they actually had Holy Days like ours, rabbis, and synagogues, everything I could perceive regarding the rest of their life had nothing in common with ours. In short, these Jews in the cold, snow, and mud seemed to me incredibly exotic: the fact that a hat with a fur brim could have become a ritual accessory among them would have made me laugh, had I dared at that time to laugh about things like that. For I could not imagine that a Jewish life could be led in any way other than with the constant complicity of the sun and the blue sky. Therefore I left these strange and faraway members of my religion alone. It was not among them that I would find the increasingly elusive object of my quest.

There remained, towering over all the others, the 'European' model. Many in the Jewish community had begun, over a century earlier, to regard this model as essential: they had adopted swimming in the sea, refrigerators and quinine, Tino Rossi, Bastille Day parades, and the Renault 4CV. But my Europe, if I may say so, was not precisely that one. It is true that I have never loved Europe so much, never dreamed of it so much, never so much believed in its countless virtues as during those years; but it was an imaginary Europe, constructed helter-skelter from materials taken from the most diverse sources. As for the true Europeans – the flesh and blood ones, the ones who, in Meknès, populated the offices of the military administration and the municipal administration, those who lived in big buildings with elevators or in fine villas with gardens in the 'new city' – I scarcely knew them, having few occasions to come in contact with them. What I did know was limited to a few very commonplace notions, based on rumor and hearsay. Stories of great successes: of the pioneers (colonists, heads of industrial or commercial enterprises, engineers, representatives of major banks, owners of newspapers) who had found, in this 'African Far West,' a country suited to their energy and ambitions. In their wake came many wheeler-dealers and less prominent speculators. The latter, it seemed to me, had only a small portion of the constructive energy that had driven their predecessors, which they used primarily to acquire the external signs of success (a car, a villa in the residential quarter called 'Meknès-Plaisance,' a cabin on the great beaches at Fedala or Temara, or a chalet in Ifrane).

The Europe of my dreams, or rather the Europe I had patiently reconstructed, the only one that seemed to me real, was that of long strolls in the stacks of the great libraries and in the labyrinth of the museums, mornings spent attending courses in university lecture halls, nights of passionate conversation on the terraces of 'literary cafes.' Apart from a few friends and professors, I did not find many people to share this utopia with me. Most of the real Europeans, preoccupied with the defense – a very poor defense, in the end – of their dominant position, were not much interested in acting as cultural models. Instead of leaning on them, I sometimes felt like shaking them violently to remind them of their duty, as if by failing to play their proper role they were putting me personally in danger, the deterioration of their image threatening finally to affect my own self-representation. In short, my quest for models sent me back to books again and only increased literature's already enormously strong grip on my everyday life.

I had therefore long been prepared – I was about to say programmed – to seek in literature the model for the book I was to write. I spent several weeks – the first ones I really devoted to my family-epic project – thinking about the subject, trying to transpose, and adapt if necessary, the structure of one or another of my favorite books. I was, of course, looking for solidly constructed books. But what a predicament I found myself in! Some new idol was constantly dethroning yesterday's idol. I will give only a few examples, the ones I remember most clearly.

I first resorted to the model that seemed to me most obvious: Proust, and the famous cathedral structure he claimed to have given his *Remembrance of Things Past*. I don't think I really understood what that meant (and I am not sure that I understand it much better now, in spite of all I've read about it), but it quickly became evident that the reference to the cathedral, erected in this way as a paradigm of the whole enterprise, would have been rather out of place in a book in which Judaism, along with Islam, were to occupy so much space. I therefore thought it wise to seek elsewhere a model more in harmony with my subject. And since it was architecture that attracted me at the moment (I opportunely recalled that Thomas Hardy had begun as an architect), since the mere idea of transforming architectural elements into textual materials delighted me, recourse to Moroccan Jewish religious buildings was obligatory.

Unfortunately, I didn't know much about the traditions and constraints in this domain. To be sure, we had long since emerged from the dark era in which Jews had been obliged to pray in secret, in which temples had to be below street level. In Meknès, however, a few traces of that former discretion seemed to have persisted. The synagogues – private buildings that pious community leaders had had built at their own expense, close to their own homes – were modest in size and usually designed to hold a few dozen believers (a hundred in the largest one). Moreover, in contrast with the mosques and churches, they avoided drawing attention to themselves by any distinctive external mark. Contemplating these modest structures was surely not what gave me a taste for the grandiose and monumental! As for the interior . . . I no longer remembered very well what it was like. I tried to recall a few of those to which I had regularly gone.

I remembered two in particular to which I had felt a strong emotional attachment. The first – rather small and cute, considered very ancient (founded by a family that had come from Spain after the expulsion) and bearing the name of Rabbi Schemaya – occupied the ground floor of a house that had belonged, at the end of the last century, to my grandparents. Its popularity derived from a custom that was as extraordinary as it was convenient: you could go to pray there at any hour of the day, for there was always (in accord with the principle – which obviously I did not know about at the time – of the nonstop movie theater) a service going on, which, for believers who could not attend the three daily offices in their usual synagogue, constituted an invaluable alternative. I held it all the more dear because it owed its rebirth, after being closed for several decades, to my grandfather Menahem, who had had it restored and decorated with beautiful sculpted woodwork. The other synagogue, which was larger and more recent (it dated from the thirties, but people were still calling it 'the new synagogue'), and of which my father had been one of the founders, was the one I had attended during my pious period. Until I entered secondary school, I went there assiduously, on Saturdays and on the major holidays: it was there that I had admired Rabbi Yossef's brilliant sermons, heard the shofar blown at Rosh Hashanah, attended, spellbound and fasting like all the faithful, the majestic service of Yom Kippur, shaken in cadence, at Sukkoth, the citron and the palm branch in its dress of multicolored silks, and seen the scrolls of the Law dance on the day of Simrath Torah.

It seemed to me that their internal arrangements were more or less analogous, and, apart from certain details, the same as would have been found in other synagogues: wooden pews in closely spaced rows, surrounding a sort of elevated dais on which the person conducting the worship stood and where the Torah was read; occupying the center of the wall facing the entrance, the Ark in which the scrolls were kept. But perhaps my memory was giving them more uniformity than they in fact had. I tried to learn more about them. My bibliographical research on the subject remained fruitless. It is true that I had carried out this research rather halfheartedly, being persuaded that there was not much to be expected from it. Therefore I abandoned that line of inquiry. Or rather I decided to move directly, in my research, to the next level. Since the modest structures of my childhood were incapable of providing the model I needed, I decided to seek it elsewhere in Jewish religious architecture. Much higher up. At the very summit of the hierarchy.

And thus it happened that I found myself examining – with a feeling still colored by my old taste for the sacred – various reconstructions of the floorplan of the Temple of Jerusalem that I had found in two big, sumptuously bound folio volumes in the École Normale's inexhaustible library. After all, this temple did look quite different from Rabbi Schemaya's synagogue! Thus I discovered all the subtleties of a way of organizing space which, being modeled on the organization of Jewish society itself, managed the transition from the most profane to the most sacred. First, the four outside porches (for the Gentiles, Women, Israelites, and Priests), then the three sections of the Temple itself, which culminated in the supreme receptacle of the Divine, the *Debir*, that is, the Holy of Holies. I spent several evenings trying to reproduce, in the structure of my book, this progression. Without success, of course. To be sure, my intention was in fact to put Gentiles (Muslims and Christians), Women (sisters, aunts, cousins and neighbors), Israelites (simple believers), as well as Priests (venerated rabbis) into my familial epic: what else could I have talked about? Wasn't it mainly that universe that I wanted to describe? But in my histories, these four categories of personages constantly mixed with one another, and I could not decently cut up my narrative in order to devote a separate section to each of them. Devastated, I had to give up what had nevertheless seemed to me, at the outset, a promising line of approach.

On leaving the architectural domain, I went back to surveying purely literary models. Since Proust had led me only to a dead-end, I thought of Joyce, with whom I had just become acquainted.

He claimed to have conceived his *Ulysses* as a simple transposition of the *Odyssey*, a claim that at the time I was not alone in taking at face value. Since I also wanted to undertake an epic, why not imitate his procedure? He himself seemed to have invited me to do so: Leopold Bloom was already a Jew; what would he lose by being given a Sephardic little brother, even if Meknès lacked, for strolling about, the charms of Dublin? I sketched out a first series of transpositions: the most charming of my female European classmates, the ones that had been the objects of my forbidden desires (Claudine, Elisabeth, or Christiane), would be very suitable Sirens, especially if I imagined them swimming naked, on a lovely day in May, in the lycée's pool; and I was sure that, in the role of the Cyclops, the terrifying Aissaouas, who devoured raw sheep, would work perfectly well. But, remembering that I was acquiring university credentials as a Latinist, I turned my gaze in a direction that seemed to me more appropriate, and tried to make my own epic a sort of *Aeneid*. The idea attracted me as a challenge. Who knows what marvels might be produced by grafting pure Latin classicism onto the often undeniably Baroque trunk of the Talmudic tree? Up to that point, in the Latin models with which I was saturated (somewhat too much for my taste, but one rarely gets off scot-free after years of university study), it was above all Cicero and Tacitus who played the principal roles: I wore myself out, in my efforts to write, by pursuing at the same time what I was told was the harmonious copiousness of the former and the sober density of the latter. Without ever catching up with them. Sweet Virgil came along at just the right time to get me out of my predicament. He allowed me to send packing these two great shades (if shades can pack, and I'm not sure they can) who, during my endless years of apprenticeship, had weighed so heavily upon me (and I know from experience that shades have weight).

And in fact I did not need to search long to make a discovery that surprised me: there was much in Virgil's work that I could easily adapt to my own ends. The role of piety (the epic and the religious could thus go hand in hand), and above all filial piety (can anyone ever forget Aeneas carrying his father on his shoulders?), the stubborn attachment to the Penates, which were taken along to the other side of the sea, the scrupulous fulfillment of a mission dictated by destiny, the accepted exile that ultimately turns out to be a return home: none of that would have been out of place in my own epic. There were also the dramatic reversals (the sojourn in Carthage with Dido, or the descent into the Underworld), for which I was sure to find satisfactory transpositions: neither love nor death could be absent from my project. Even the endless wars with Turnus, Mezentius, and other minor kings and tribal leaders – with whom, at first, I didn't know what to do – which, it seemed to me, could be adapted to the conflicts endemic in the last years of independent Morocco. Finally I had, thanks to Virgil, a convenient way of reconciling the two types of novels that Raymond Queneau distinguished (the *Iliad*s and the *Odyssey*s), since the *Aeneid* was both. In the euphoria arising from these discoveries, I set about reworking my outline in order to make each book of Virgil's poem correspond to a chapter of my novel. But the more I worked at it, the more complicated things seemed to me. Too many episodes, too many characters were left over. My later efforts with *The Divine Comedy* and Dante's circles of hell, then with Flaubert's *Sentimental Education*, and finally with various other novels (Conrad, Melville, Kafka, and Nizan in succession) got nowhere. I had taken the wrong path once again.

To the point that I started to wonder whether it wouldn't be better to seek my model in a register other than fiction. Durrell had constructed his *Alexandria Quartet* as a novelistic transposition of Einstein's theories. Why not follow his example by choosing, for instance in philosophy, a well-structured system to be used as a secret underpinning? The whole work would be merely a transposition or projection, in the form of anecdotes selected precisely for their emblematic character, of this basic theoretical nucleus. I immediately eliminated Descartes as being insufficiently epic and turned instead toward the Germans. But a few nights spent in the company of Schelling and Schopenhauer were enough to dissuade me.

Disappointed, I returned to architecture, but from an entirely different angle. In order to avoid the arbitrariness that had paralyzed my first attempts, this time I would choose my models not from buildings foreign to my subject and about which, in addition, I had only a vague idea, but rather in the main buildings that were to be mentioned in my book. Taking my inspiration – very freely – from the ancient arts of memory, which advise orators to associate the parts of their discourse with the architectural elements of a familiar building, I amused myself by regrouping everything around a few selected places sacred to the family, still heavily freighted, for me and for my family, with memories, regrets, or at least dreams. Places that seemed to me moreover capable of providing excellent titles for my chapters, and even, should the work end up taking on larger proportions, a possibility I did not in any way exclude (in my moments of optimism, I already saw looming a veritable Sephardic *Rougon-Macquart* series, nothing less), volume titles: a significant advantage for someone preparing to write a family saga.

Thus I had arranged the whole of my narrative as a tour with at least four stages. The reader would enter, at a deliberate pace, through 'Jacob's Garden,' a miraculous island of greenery – whose small size had made Pierre Loti smile – alongside the wretched misery of the old mellah in Meknès, in the 1880s. Between its high walls (on which arbors were painted) and little orange trees it would include everything I could find on the life of Jacob Ohana, the origins of his fortune, his close friendship with Sultan Mulay Hassan, the last great representative sovereign of independent Morocco. Then the reader would be transported to Rabat and linger in the various apartments, in the various rooms, systematically examined and described, along with their furnishings and the people who lived in them, of 'The Apartment Building.' Of course, this apartment building would be Menahem's; the story of the beginnings of the Protectorate, marked by the collapse of the structures of the 'Sherifian Empire' and the emergence of a new society, would provide the framework for the epic of Menahem and the maternal branch of the family up to the beginning of the 1930s. Then the reader would return to Meknès in order to piously reflect, amidst the springtime explosion of wildflowers in the new cemetry, on 'Mimoun's Tomb.' In this way would be taken up, in a retrospective form, the chronicle of the paternal branch: the role of Mimoun in the original development of his city's Jewish community and the story of the creation of a new neighborhood would be the main points, which would be rounded out by a few ancillary narratives about other people (uncles, aunts, or cousins) linked to this branch of the family. Then the reader would reach, at the end of his journey, 'The New House,' where I would finally be able to unload, and at length, the accumulation of accessory details inopportunely encumbering my memory: the heavy wrought-iron door, the rooms lined up one after the other, and, in the middle of the garden, the water fountain shimmering in its star-shaped basin. It was there that would take place, around my parents and amid my brothers and sisters, the most significant episodes of our family life, at least so far as my memory allowed me to reconstruct them.

My relationships – whether direct or indirect, real or imaginary – with each of these places had never really ceased. I therefore believed I could, without too much difficulty, take advantage of their intense symbolic and emotive value. However, I quickly saw that this kind of division of my material, despite the attractions of its apparent logic, was not tenable. This was simply because my so-called stages were not stages at all. First, they excluded whole aspects of the family past, remote (everything that antedated Jacob) as well as near (everything that came after the new house), which I had no intention of jettisoning; next, being very dissimilar in content as well as in duration, they introduced among the parts of the book (or worse yet, if the work took on the desired dimensions, among the volumes of the saga) an unacceptable disproportion; finally, the heroes and the events of each of these stages were far too imbricated for it to be possible really to separate them. My architectural construction thus collapsed like a house of cards, and I had to bid farewell to my idea of a tour: obviously, my projected interlacings could not dwell within such a linear structure.

No, clearly, it was to a literary model that I needed, once again (and as always) to return. Why not the pages of the Talmud that I had formerly seen in my father's hands, or during my summer lessons in the Rabbinical school's big building? With their wisely distributed lines and columns and differing alphabets, they presented, at a single glance, five or six distinct texts. Wasn't this the ideal model for me, that of a book in which were juxtaposed, or rather interlaced, several series of texts, differing and yet related? I decided to keep this venerable schema in mind in order to explore at leisure its possible developments. I had the feeling that its fecundity would be greatly increased if I succeeded in combining it with others coming from a different tradition.

All these unsuccessful attempts did not, however, seem to me useless. As I moved from one failure to another, I was defining more and more precisely my goal. What I was looking for, in fact, was a support, an armature, a hard mass around which I could execute the numerous variations I had in mind, while unreservedly indulging my taste for fleeting allusions, picturesque memories, veiled revelations – in short, all the miniscule and irreplaceable details without which my pages might well ring hollow.

At the same time, I dreamed of a simple language, consisting of the most familiar, and even the most worn-out expressions. Of sentences that would succeed, through their very transparency, in propagating the impalpable messages of which I felt myself the fortunate bearer: the fragrance, so particular, of the little chicken livers that quietly sizzled on the charcoal stove, on Friday afternoons, and their taste when they began to melt on my tongue, radiating their warmth throughout my mouth like little bits of the embers; or the sensation of being slightly burned that I got, deep in my throat, from the eau-de-vie (tasting of dried figs) which my father allowed me to drink with him on certain holiday mornings, after returning from the synagogue.

I had not yet written the slightest chapter before I already experienced the tyranny of the work to be created, the torments and struggles of bringing it to birth. I therefore decided to stop looking for models and to set out, for once, without any clear goal in view.

UNCERTAIN ANCESTORS

Into the cave of my people
Plunging my nocturnal steps,
I counted my ancestors
In accord with their old law.
– Alfred de Vigny, 'L'Esprit pur'

I started with the most pressing question: where, and especially when, should I make my family epic begin? To my great surprise, finding an answer to that question did not take too long. In fact, as a lover of antiquity I was resolved to go back as far as possible. There is no proper epic without an invigorating dive into the past. Yes, it would be necessary to gambol about in the most distant epochs, dip with both hands into the most ancient history's stock of life, and resuscitate a cohort of more or less forgotten shades, to awaken these distant and mysterious heroes whose presence was already haunting me even when I still knew nothing about them.

I glimpsed, of course, the danger to which this choice would expose me: the most ancient periods were also likely to be the most lacking in credible family references, in reliable documents. Far too often (in any case, more often than I would have wished), I had to be content with vague bits and pieces, questionable fragments. That did not discourage me. After all, I was in a position to know what subtle forgeries are at work in most narratives of origin, how much the authors of such works extrapolate, combine, and construct on the basis of formless bits of debris, how they are willing to accept a little myth or legend when they need it, so sure are they, in doing this, that they are satisfying the desire – hardly concealed – of the majority of their readers. In order to carry out my own movement back into family time, I was prepared to adopt these tried and true methods. I was forced to do so, moreover, by the meagerness and nature of the material I had at hand: a few proper names.

This was not the first time I had had to deal with people's names. According to my mother's stories, 'what's your name?' (which became, in my childish pronunciation, a comminatory 'wutyouname?') had been one of my obsessions as soon as I had learned to talk: I asked the same question of every adult I met and was not always satisfied with the reply. I obviously don't remember that very ancient period, but I do know how much I was troubled, later on, when I discovered that there was not necessarily a perfect congruence between a person and his name: even though I was considered a calm and rather sweet child, one day I had flown into a violent rage, right in the middle of a holiday meal, against one of my uncles, whom I called a liar and ultimately a thief, because he insisted, in spite of all logic, in telling me that his name was David, whereas I knew very well that David was my father . . . a little later, it was the inverse problem that bothered me: when I noticed that a single person could be designated, at different times, by different appellations. Not only because of the fad for diminutives, which transformed André into Dédé, Joseph into Jojo, Simone into Mimi, Lucien into Lulu. But rather because, among my first playmates, all those who had adopted a European first name (the one they used in everyday life) had also, since their birth (or more precisely, for the males, since the day of their circumcision, because the collation of the forename and the ablation of the foreskin were merely two phases of the same operation), another first name, a Hebraic one. A first name which had moreover become, with time, a sort of semiclandestine expression, vaguely shameful, and which one was not at all inclined to reveal, except in a small group of friends, and with a conniving smile; it took its revenge only in the majestic framework of the religious ceremonies; there, recovering all its sacred, original power, it relegated the other name to the rank of a frivolous ornament, and it alone was valid.

I was again to encounter these problems of noncongruence in my later struggles with patronymics, and chiefly with my own. However, everything had started off rather well. My mother, in her first stories, describing the marriages contracted in the family over several generations, threaded her way expertly through the labyrinth of the Ohanas and the Oliels, the Corcos and the Coriats, the Berdugos and the Toledanos, the Amars and the Attars, the Azoulays and the Aflalos, the Azoguis and the Addis, not to mention the Benazras, the Benarroshes, the Bensimons, and the Benchimols. I got winded just trying to keep up with her. But this abundance of names belonging to related families (and she never forgot to say that they were 'among the most honorable') flattered me. I considered it an indirect recognition awarded our own name, which was thus endowed, through its perpetuation and through the quality of its alliances, with a central role: like a main branch in the great, leafy community tree. This had caused me to conceive, when I was not yet ten years old, an enormous pride that seemed to me fully legitimate.

Alas, on this delicate point, I soon had to recant, and return, astonished and then sheepish, to a more accurate assessment of things. I was not long in discovering – it happened, for the first time, in the lycée – the effect that could be produced on a European audience by the harmonious collocation of consonants and vowels that was supposed to designate me. All I had to do was to utter my name, for instance on coming into a new classroom, or on going to sign up for the theatergoers' club (*La Scène française*) or the music lovers' club (*Les Jeunesses musicales de France*), to feel that I was immediately placed, with no possibility of appeal, on the other side of an invisible dividing line. Later on, at the time of my first flirtations, it was even worse: I could not help seeing the embarrassment, clumsily concealed, of certain French girlfriends when they had to introduce me to their parents: at such moments, I had the painful sensation of being, in my name (with its rebarbative redoubling of syllables beginning with *b*) shut up in a sort of prison, and I am sure that there immediately appeared on my face – behind the expected smile – the tormented look of those who know that they have been laid bare. Constantly on my guard, I acquired the habit of revealing only parsimoniously – that is, only when it was unavoidable – my patronymic, which thus joined in an embarrassed semiclandestinity my Hebraic forename (in so doing, I adopted without knowing it a social attitude, the dissimulation of the proper name, which I later discovered to be rather widespread – but for entirely different reasons than mine – in the societies that used to be called primitive). Just one example: when I was still working on my project – finally aborted – of writing a Racinian tragedy, I had thought for a long time about the title page, which was to appear in this form, carefully written in my hand:

The Death of Hannibal

Heroic Tragedy
in five acts

By Monsieur Marcel B.

I had not thought it useful to put anything on the title page beyond my first name and the initial of my patronymic. Not from modesty, nor from a precocious preference for anonymity. But rather because I did not like, in this case, the excessive transparency of my name. It seemed to me that these few syllables, revealing my origin as surely as in other times a yellow star or a pointed hat would have revealed it, threatened to cast unjust suspicion on the noble writings at whose head they would appear. Hence I had not hesitated, in order to ensure that my tragedy would at least have a chance to find readers, to practice a radical onomastic purification. Later, in Paris, the problem grew still more complicated. The name that up to this point pointed only to Jewishness began to convey a more ambiguous message. It indicated first of all and especially a North African origin, which was, for many French people, synonymous with Arabic or Muslim. Thus I again found myself, more than once, embarrassed and misunderstood, not always daring to disabuse those who, erring with regard to my religious affiliation, talked to me in a way they surely would not have talked to a Jew.

One can thus imagine how concerned I was about having to handle, even for epic or novelistic ends, such an explosive subject matter. My concern was further increased by my discovery, in an esoteric work that gave the meaning of certain Semitic roots (I have lost the reference, but it was perhaps by Fabre d'Olivet), which I had not found encouraging. About *'ab,* it said this: 'The *'ain,* a sign of the material meaning, combined through contraction with the root *ab,* the symbol of all desire and all fruitfulness, constitutes a root that characterizes the material center and, in a less general sense, anything that is condensed, thickens, becomes heavy and obscure . . . ; the Arabic *'ab* signifies assuming a burden.' Finding, at the very threshold of my genealogical research, and consubstantially linked with my patronymic, this atmosphere of heaviness and obscurity, did not bode well . . .

As I set out, my baggage consisted of no more than four names (Benabou, Ohana, Azoulay, and Oliel), which were going to be the four leading cards in my hand. They were distributed this way: Benabou (also written Ben Abou or Ben Abbou) is the name of my two grandfathers, who were brothers; Ohana belongs to my maternal grandmother, and thus to the father, grandfather, and so on, of this grandmother), Azoulay belongs to my paternal grandmother (and thus to the father, grandfather, and so on, of this grandmother); as for Oliel, it was shared by two of my great-grandmothers (they were sisters; one of them had married my great-grandfather Benabou, the other my great-grandfather Ohana). My family tree thus has an unusual peculiarity: at certain points, it closes rather than opening up. Although I had, like everyone, two parents and two pairs of grandparents, I had only three pairs of great-grandparents (instead of the normal four) and five pairs of great-great-grandparents (instead of the normal eight). Beyond this, I had little reliable information on the subject. How, with such meager equipment, was I to conquer the most remote familial past and bring back the flamboyant episodes that were indispensable for getting my epic off the ground?

Not being a genealogical expert – and not much caring, at that time, to become one, for that would have slowed me up – I had adopted a few simple rules that were to become my weapons in hunting down my ancestors.

The first of these, which I named the 'homonymic weapon,' involved considering as potential ancestors all Moroccan Jews who bore one of the four basic names – as attested by some document or other that had come to my attention – on the condition that they had lived before the appearance of these names in my family. Thus it seemed to me legitimate to capture all the Ohanas or Oliels that lived before my great-grandparents.

The second weapon was more audacious. I called it the 'homophonic weapon.' Observing that a single name can appear, from one period to another, in differing forms, spellings, and transcriptions (the transition from Semitic to Latin modes of writing not always taking place without loss), I decided to claim anyone whose name phonetically resembled, even remotely, one of my basic names. Thus I was able to constitute, around the single name Benabou, a nebula of names that included, whether or not they were preceded by the *Ben* that indicates descent, *Abu, Abo* or *Abbou, Ebo* or *Ebbo*, as well as the occasional rare *Ebu*.

Having thus set out on the path of irredentism, I was led to introduce a third rule, which I called the 'diasporic weapon': taking into account the Jew's extreme geographical mobility (which was, as everyone knows, more often coerced than voluntary, but that's another story), I resolved not to limit myself to the Moroccan family lines and to extend my search to other parts of the Jewish world. With regard to this last rule, it is clear that I was already harboring, without realizing it, a retrospective desire to escape, the longing to break off a familial conversation with Morocco that had already gone on too long.

I had to take only one more step to break out into the open. The 'diasporic weapon' set me directly, and in a more or less natural manner, on the path to a still more powerful piece of hunting equipment, which I called the 'ecumenical weapon.' Given the frequency, in the annals of Judaism, of conversions (forced or voluntary; again, that's another story), I felt authorized to extend my search for ancestors beyond the Jewish community. Why should Islamic or Christian Abous be forever excluded from the family circle? I was already counting up, like the milkmaid in La Fontaine's fable, the advantages this would have for my work. On the Islamic side, I would thereby recuperate, without striking a blow, my handsome Muslim chief riding, at the head of his horsemen, straight out of Delacroix's sketches. On the Christian side, two fine catches. One emerged quite naturally: Edmond About. Could I neglect a writer who was said to be a second Voltaire, even if he was not quite a match for his predecessor? The other one forced me to push the homophonic rule a little further: the illustrious Venetian, Cardinal Bembo. How could I not enlist such a man among our ranks? Three characteristics seemed to me to make him eminently close and dear: a fervent book lover, he had collected a magnificent library; a fervent lover of Latin, he refused to read his breviary for fear of spoiling the purity of his style; a fervent lover of women, he had been Lucretia Borgia's paramour.

My very first attempts were more fruitful than I had dared hope. It is true that, in order to correct the liberalism of my four initial rules, I had been prudent enough not to extend my field of exploration too far back in time. I was especially concerned that my credibility, to which I attached great importance, not be destroyed by imitating the enthusiastic (but imprudent) learned men of the Middle Ages and Renaissance who had not hesitated to seek, and of course to find (at the cost of having to perform acrobatic feats that now make philologists smile), for each people, for each of the reigning families of Europe, eponymous ancestors among the leading heroes of Greek and Roman epic. Thus, eschewing the opportunity to make my own legend begin with some patriarch or Biblical prophet (an option others, better served by onomastics, did not fail to take advantage of), I limited myself to searching among the later periods of Jewish history. Naturally, I turned toward the Talmud: according to what I knew about it – very little, to tell the truth – it contained so much information, answered so many questions – the oddest as well as the most unexpected – that it might also, after all, offer a path for my genealogical quest.

Immediately, having made an initial – and very timid – incursion into the French translation of the *Jerusalem Talmud* (a few volumes produced by Moses Schwab, which were quietly sleeping in one of the most peaceful and sunlit corners of the École Normale's library, lost among countless works on Christian theology, in particular the compact battalion of the *Proceedings of the Council of Trent*, in Latin), I found, with a cackle of pleasure, the mention of a personage named Elisha Ben Abouya. Better still, the learned translator, who devoted a few words to him in the introduction, alluded – and this surprised me at the time – to his 'religious skepticism,' and presented him as 'an ancestor of Faust'! My guiding star had thus led me to quite an old rascal. I quickly discovered – my surprise growing as I learned more and more – his strong personality and his singular itinerary.

He had been, in the Judea of the second century of the Common Era, a famous sage, the equal of Judaism's greatest figures in that period, known and recognized by everyone (even prostitutes). But being too much of a freethinker to accept tradition blindly, and nourishing, moreover, a passion for Greek philosophy and poetry, he was overcome by rebellious impulses and doubts when it seemed to him that things in this world were not proceeding in accord with what is written in the Torah. This revelation led him very far, too far, in the view of his contemporaries: he was on the path of dissidence, even of apostasy. Thus the man who had been a great master in the study of the Torah had not hesitated to turn young people away from it (he advised them instead – what a sacrilege! – to learn a trade) and to preach the pure and simple abandonment of certain practices that were considered the very basis of Jewish religious life, pushing his challenge so far as to openly violate the sacrosanct Sabbath rest by riding around, on horseback, in front of a man who had been one of his most faithful disciples. He was, of course, expelled from the community. To the point that the Talmudic texts, having put a sort of taboo on this heretic's name, usually designated him only by the surname Aher, that is, *the Other*.

I accepted all that as a veritable windfall. Having set out precisely in search of what made me different, could I have dreamed of an ancestor more attractive than this great *Other*, this archetypal *Other*, whom a very opportune stroke of luck, closely resembling an act of Providence, was allowing me to put into the excessively meager hand I had to play? He was the first and most illustrious victim of the combined effects of the 'homophonic weapon' and the 'diasporic weapon': I decreed that the final syllable of his name was a mere intruder, and thus subject to the rigors of apocope, and, repeating the act that in Genesis had transformed Sarai into Sara, I proceeded without further ado to the immediate ablation of this superadded appendage. In this way, Ben Abouya became a very acceptable Ben Abou. He was promptly enthroned as a member of the family. Not with a marginal or subalternate status, like that of a distant cousin or assumed relative, but really and truly elevated to the rank of the founder of the dynasty: others had taken the Atreides or the Aeneades as their heroes; it was reserved for me to sing the solemn saga of the Benabouyades.

One point still bothered me, however: apart from his intellectual choices as a rationalist and a freethinker, which had led him to take on the thankless role of the one who sobers up, shakes up, and cleans up, I knew next to nothing about my new ancestor's private life. Now, there was no question of my presenting the reader with an epic, a familial novel, without a few intimate details, and if possible moving ones, concerning the person of the founder, his amorous or marital problems. Can one imagine the *Iliad* without Andromache, the *Odyssey* without Penelope, or the *Aeneid* without Dido? I had to fill in this gap. I had already found, in my Talmudic readings, a scene that seemed to me promising: Ben Abouya picking, right in the middle of the Sabbath, a radish to give to a prostitute he desired. Maybe I could take this incident and make a fable out of it, something like 'The Rabbi, the Radish, and the Whore'? Or else I could inflate it and make it the symbol of a love life resolutely turning its back on family values? But I was not yet mature enough for that much irreverence. Moreover, if I wanted Ben Abouya to be the root of my family tree, I absolutely had to endow him with a true family; in addition, I knew that he had had a daughter, perhaps several daughters, who were for a time reduced to beggary.

On reflection, it seemed to me that it would be a good idea to attribute to him, in this domain, experiences analogous to those of his peers and contemporaries, the great Talmudic masters (some of whom – the good people who stayed up all night at Passover – had earlier served me as an excuse for my nocturnal reading). What could be more touching than the love of Rabbi Akiba and his wife Rachel? The beautiful Rachel was the daughter of a particularly rich man in Jerusalem for whom the future Rabbi Akiba had worked in his youth; she gave up without regret the soft comfort of the paternal house to secretly marry Rabbi Akiba. All her impecunious husband had to offer her was his poverty and his straw pallet; but very tenderly, every morning he picked the bits of straw, one by one, from Rachel's hair. When he decided, rather late, to go away to study the Torah, he left her alone, and she had no recourse, in order to provide for herself, other than to sell her beautiful hair. But when he came back, and became famous and sought out, he modestly declared, before the disciples crowding around him: 'It is to her that my knowledge and yours belong.' As for Rabbi Yosse Hagalili, he was much less lucky in choosing a wife. He was saddled with a cantankerous shrew, whom he could not leave because he lacked the money to pay the sum specified in his *ketuba* (marriage contract). Fortunately, his friend Rabbi Eleazar ben Azaria, who was very rich, took pity on him and gave him the necessary funds. But the ex-wife did not make good use of the money. In her hands, the money quickly melted away. Moreover, the husband she had married after her divorce went blind. Then Rabbi Yosse magnanimously took care of both of them until they died (irresistibly, his generosity made me think of my Aunt Zahra). As for Rabbi

Tarfon, his problem was not exactly a conjugal problem. In fact, he was in love with his own daughter-in-law. This seemed to be known in the Talmudic hinterland, since it had even become the object of jokes made by his peers. That is why, fearing that he would succumb to this illicit passion, the good rabbi begged his disciples to keep him under constant surveillance. All this provided me with an interesting spectrum of amorous attitudes and conjugal situations, some of which anticipated in an odd way the ones I had encountered in my research on my close relatives; it remained only for me to figure out the best way to slip them into the pages I was firmly resolved to devote to Ben Abouya.

The same friendly Providence that had allowed me to furnish myself with such an ancestor and to endow him with such adventures soon set me on a path leading to another great figure, that of Schlomo Ben 'Abou, who was certainly not unworthy of playing, alongside Ben Abouya, the role of a brilliant second. For if he smelled less of sulfur, he was certainly unusual in his own way. I had seen him unexpectedly arrive in a Berber village in southern Morocco, Ifrane (also called Oufrane), which had formerly been, it was said, the center of a little Jewish kingdom. His tombstone, which had been rediscovered in what seems to be the oldest Jewish cemetery in Morocco, bears an inscription, dating perhaps from the sixth century (being prudent, I avoided questioning the plausibility of that dating, which seemed to me pretty old), describing him as 'a miracle worker.' He appeared at the right moment. Thanks to him, I was going to be able to give myself my first Moroccan roots, and I was happy to tell myself that they went down into the heart of the Berber world. For in my view, my thaumaturge could only belong to that ancient fringe of North African Jews descended from the Berber tribes converted to Judaism at the end of the Roman period. This was a population whose extraordinary fate (there had never been, so far as I knew, a plethora of mass conversions in the history of Judaism) interested me. I couldn't help comparing this conversion with a curious tradition, which I had just come across in certain Latin authors of North Africa including Augustine himself: according to the latter, the Berbers were descendants of the Canaanites – former inhabitants of Palestine – who were supposed to have fled Canaan as Joseph and the Hebrews advanced toward it. Juxtaposing these two facts, it seemed to me amusing to see the sign of an intervention, ironic to say the least, on the part of Providence, since when they became Jews, the Hebraic imprint their ancestors had tried to flee had apparently caught up with some of these Berbers, in spite of the centuries and seas separating them! Connecting myself, by way of a miracle worker, with these quasi-miraculous people in Jewish history did not displease me at all. I was very happy to annex this new ancestor and to give him a place in accord with his merits.

He fit well, I thought, into the throng of saints whom Moroccan Jews had always loved and venerated and whose tombs, which were regularly visited, became the goal of pilgrimages. There were several hundred of them, it was said, especially in the southern part of the country, in the regions that still remained for me no more than simple geographical expressions: Souss, the High Atlas, Tafilalelt. The only one I knew about was also the most famous and the most consulted, Rabbi Amram Ben Diwan. We had gone at least once as a family to visit his tomb, near Oeuzzane, on the occasion of Hillulah. An unforgettable event. The car trip, in the already oppressive heat of late spring, had been long and difficult. We had left early. The car, heavily loaded, lurched around the curves. Squeezed between my father and my mother, I had fallen asleep, when suddenly the car stopped in the middle of the road, which was fortunately deserted. An enormous swarm of crickets had just descended upon us. They were everywhere, hundreds of them, on the windshield, the hood, the fenders, the roof of the old Chevrolet. We were able to start up again only when the swarm – having quickly annihilated the surrounding vegetation – came together again. From the pilgrimage itself, I recalled only a few images, a few odors. It was, in the midst of a mountainous setting far more imposing than my familiar Zerhoun, a sort of untidy caravansary: a collection of tents, each of them sheltering a large family, amid flies and beggars. During the day, there was a crazy, kermis-like atmosphere, with singing, dancing, and music, and a strong odor of barbecued mutton rising up everywhere. But at night, the whole life of the strange encampment came together around the saint's tomb, which was transformed into a giant inferno: a swarming and noisy mass of men and women thrown together, constantly tossing candles on it, begging the saint to grant their prayers amid the odor, at first sweet but later nauseating, of melted wax.

I was therefore sure that my miracle-working rabbi would be warmly welcomed into the family, by my mother in particular. Always worried about us, she tried every system, every method, every remedy that might provide the most effective protection for our health. She had great confidence in medical science (a confidence that in my humble, retrospective opinion the local representatives of that noble discipline, despite their efforts, did not always deserve); nevertheless, in benign cases, she was often willing to resort to the most ancient home remedies: onion, wild thyme, and fenugreek were the uncontested stars of her pharmacopoeia; sometimes, calling on a saint, provided that he was the right one, or a few heartfelt incantations to ward off the 'evil eye,' might suffice. Thus she would certainly be reassured by the presence of a thaumaturge in her genealogy, even a few centuries away. One could always appeal to him in cases where the usual intercessors were too slow in providing the thousand and one favors daily asked of them. And, who knows, it might be that, flattered to thus be called upon again after too long a period of retirement, he would agree to work for us, his direct descendants, some genuine miracle, worthy of those of former times. I even imagined that we might one day establish a festival in his honor that would serve to bring together, on a certain date, all of us who recognized him as our ancestor.

In spite of these promising roots, the rest of the tree proved more difficult to establish. On the Bénabou side, there were enormous gaps. I found no one else before the eighteenth century. 'It certainly isn't the tree of Jesse, rather the tree of *je-ne-sais-pas*, I was told by a friend who was also concerned with family tree questions. I was forced to leap over a few obscure centuries – at least a dozen – to find myself again in Palestine, but this time in Safed, the city of the Kabalists, where a little eighteenth-century synagogue (which can be visited) bears the name of Rabbi Salomon Abou, that is, the same name as that of the thaumaturge of Oufrane. A fine example of onomastic fidelity, to be sure, but this immense hiatus obviously did not help me. I would have preferred that no piece be missing from my genealogical puzzle, that no century escaped my apologetic vigilance. How was I going to properly populate what I had immediately named 'the first intermediary period'? The solution was quickly found: since I no longer had any Benabous to write about, it was time for me to turn to the allied family lines, those of the Ohanas, the Oliels, and the Azoulays, which I had not yet explored.

On the Ohana side, I found myself sent back to Oufrane, where the family seems to have come from, but the first representative I was able to dig up, a rabbi who had emigrated to Safed, was not anterior to the beginning of the eighteenth century.

On the Oliel side, I got no further: I couldn't go back beyond the second half of the eighteenth century, with a rabbi of Sefrou,

Rabbi Joshua, who was very likely to have been the grandfather of my two great-grandmothers.

The Azoulay path turned out to be the most productive. The Azoulays were among the families that had taken refuge in Morocco after the expulsion of the Jews from Spain in 1492. They were therefore a link of capital importance, because through them I could make the connection with Spanish Judaism. I had at first hesitated to make this retrospective grafting. My feelings with regard to these expelled Jews were not, at the time, without a certain ambiguity. I admired on faith – I hadn't looked into the matter myself – the positive points everyone saw in them: their high cultural level, acquired over the centuries of happy coexistence with Christian and Muslim intellectuals in Granada or Córdoba, the beneficent role they played everywhere where they established themselves (Montaigne, Spinoza, and Disraeli, their descendants, were certainly not second cousins to be disdained). What bothered me was the conditions under which they arrived in Morocco: these did not seem to me sufficiently glorious for an epic. After all, I said to myself, they had settled in a land they had not really chosen: neither the mildness of the climate, nor the beauty of the landscape, nor the hospitality of the local populations had drawn or kept them there, but only the impossibility of going any further, the necessity of putting an end to their flight out of the lost Iberian paradise. I also knew that once they had settled there, these Spanish families, more cultivated and more refined, had long insisted on showing their superiority with regard to local Jews, and I saw in them a haughtiness that shocked me. Fortunately, I was not long in learning as well that, in certain cities, such as Fez or Meknès, the two groups had fused, and in the end that was the most important thing.

I therefore decided to follow that line. It was to endow me with an important series of direct lineages. Moreover, it allowed me to postulate the presence, among my ancestors on that side, of other Spanish families with whom the Azoulays had earlier been able to connect themselves. This was the case, for instance, of a few Toledanos, Berdugos, Marcianos, and Malkas, who added further, precious branches to my genealogical tree. I had a particular predilection for Talmudists, Kabalists, and rabbis of all sorts: they permitted me to remain in the ethereal universe I had immediately marked off by the choice of my first ancestors. Nevertheless, I sometimes wondered if all these newcomers would have been overjoyed by my attempts to bring them back to light. 'After all,' they would have answered had I had the opportunity to ask them, 'history is useless for people who have devoted their lives to the essential thing, that is, to meditation on the Torah.' But that scruple didn't hold me back for long.

The other side of this coin was that with such a burgeoning of potential ancestors, the genealogical situation was completely reversed: the obscure centuries were not so deserted as I had feared; on the contrary, they were filled with a dense crowd, and were for that reason difficult to handle. There was no longer any possibility of following a precise line and still less of drawing up a genuine family tree. Such a task, even supposing that it were possible, far surpassed my abilities as an amateur, unskilled genealogist. This was hard for me to accept. But afterward, what a relief! Henceforth, I was free to choose the ancestors I liked, without worrying too much about the links that might (or might not) connect them with me.

Thanks to the various repertories, inventories, and catalogs I was able – not without difficulty – to consult, I garnered a stock of names: a diverse group of people, to be sure, but ones who had deserved to remain in our collective memory and who had thereby won the right to play an honorable role in my epic. Then I set out to find a principle that would permit me to classify them.

First came the ones whose names had been preserved by history, by world history: the ministers, counselors, and ambassadors of certain kings. I noted down, all jumbled together, Maimranes, Toledanos, Benattars. They had served, with varying success, the terrible Moulay Ismael. I resolved not to omit a single one of their lofty feats.

Next came, in serried ranks, all the others.

Some of these presented themselves already bearing the stamp of genuine tragic heroes. It would be easy to integrate them into my story. They would occupy a place that has never remained vacant for long in the history of many past Jewish communities, the place of martyrs. Hence, just after having noted with great surprise the all-too-lengthy series of massacres, like that of Judah Afriat and his sixty men at Oufrane, I had been brought up short by two other figures whom I less expected: two pure young maidens. This was a real windfall, once again! I immediately wrote down their story. A story of love, violence, and death, as is only proper. Through a strange coincidence, both of the girls had been the victims, at about the same time (the first half of the last century), of their excessive beauty and their fidelity to their religion. One of them, Solica Hatchouel, was convicted and executed for continuing to declare that she was a Jew, although a Muslim neighbor, a rejected suitor, claimed to have converted her to Islam; the other, Esther Abrabanel (not knowing her first name, I had, on my own authority, given her the name Esther), whom her fiancé had to kill with his own hand to prevent her from being kidnapped by the Sultan's henchmen. In these stories I found all the necessary ingredients for the 'tragedies of the mellah' that I proposed to write later (after having completed my family epic), as a sequel to Zangwill's classic *Ghetto Tragedies*, and whose main lines I immediately laid down: heroines and heroes torn between conflicting duties, even full of doubt or fear, great moments of hope preceding moments of disillusionment, soberly dramatic dialogues, and, to give the whole thing the indispensable antique touch, the sorrowing presence, in the background, of the whole community, sharing the woes of the unfortunate protagonists.

I was first concerned with the fate of the beautiful Solica. I already imagined myself reconstructing, scene by scene, all the stages of her drama, from the first glance (that of a chaste adolescent) exchanged with her admirer and future accuser, up to her public beheading, reserving, obviously, a privileged place for her trial, which was held in Fez in 1834 before the Sultan Moulay Abderrahman. In fact, I went much further. I imagined, carried away by the spirit of the time, making out of this prosecution of an adolescent, who hadn't done anything but be herself (that is, young, beautiful, and Jewish), something Brechtian: the incarnation of the fundamental injustice of societies. When Solica was sacrificed – tortured, significantly, on the Sultan's own orders – what was this but the powerful of this world crushing a solitary and fragile individual who resists the forces that are trying to make her renounce her very self?

As for Esther, her story seemed to call for a different treatment, for it was situated in a familial and historical context that presented opportunities I simply couldn't pass up. The familial context: the name of Abrabanel went back to one of the most illustrious representatives of the Spanish Golden Age, Don Isaac, who was both a famed Talmudic scholar and minister to Alfonso V of Portugal, and later to Ferdinand and Isabella of Spain. The historical context: the events took place at a time when Sultan Moulay Abderrahman needed money to support Emir Abdelkader in his battle against the French; it happened that Esther's father, Judah, was one of the wealthiest men in the Jewish community in Marrakech and thus was one of those on whom great burdens are placed in such circumstances. It was while the Sultan's men were searching Judah's house, looking for hidden treasure, that they found Esther and tried to kidnap her. This discreet intrusion of an episode from French colonial history on the backstage of my family epic was obviously not displeasing to me.

Right next to these tragic heroes – but distinct from them – I placed another category of characters. Their adventures, which began tragically, turned out favorably in the end. I intended, of course, to integrate them into my planned epic. I even began to think up some titles for their stories, adopting the oriental style, which seemed to me appropriate in this case.

– 'The Story of the Saintly Man Who Saved His Community by Making the Body of the Slain Prince Talk' (Mordecai Benattar, date unknown, fourteenth to fifteenth centuries).

– 'The Story of the Rabbi Taken Down from the Gallows by Five of his Students Disguised as the Sultan's Soldiers' (Samuel Danino, under the bloody reign of Moulay Yazid, in 1790).

– 'The Story of the Goldsmith Who Made a Gold Bracelet to Confound the False Prophet Persecuting the Jews' (Jacob Belahsen, second half of the eighteenth century).

This was the classical schema of the 'just man saved' or the 'wicked man punished' through supernatural intervention. A schema that was reassuring for these communities that had been so often tested: they greatly needed, in their helplessness before their persecutors, to rely from time to time on concrete signs of divine protection that often had a tendency to remain purely theoretical. But it was a precious schema for the storyteller, because these miraculous episodes would introduce into my narrative the indispensable dose of mystery and the supernatural without which there has never been, since Homer, any epic worthy of the name.

Martyrs and saviors – it was clear that these were two categories to emphasize, for their obvious literary virtues. But in my pouch I had many more ancestors discovered according to my methods. These were located in a less elevated register, closer to the anecdote or folk tale. They nevertheless afforded me some attractive figures. How could I avoid making room for Samuel Ben Ouaïch, the old rabbi who, armed only with his cane, drove a lioness out of the synagogue, where she had disturbed his prayers? Or for those dear visionaries, whose spiritual adventure contrasted in such a charming way with the devotion to routine and conformity often attributed to the community: Joseph Abensour, who did not hesitate to claim to be a prophet and to announce the return of the alleged Messiah, Shabatai Tsevi; Moshe Edery, who believed – like many others – that he had tracked down the lost Ten Tribes; and Jacob Abehsera, who died in Egypt and whose tomb was visited by both Jewish and Muslim pilgrims?

Finally, I had several figures of another kind, and of another stamp as well, such as Joseph Buzaglo, the diplomat who sought in vain to negotiate the sale of Tangier to France, or David Azencott, an interpreter at the French consulate in Tangier who became a close friend of Alexandre Dumas. These men had been able to find a place in their century and remain in people's memories for reasons other than religious ones. Open to the outside world, bearers of the future, they seemed to me not inappropriate additions to my lovely genealogical structure.

I was ultimately not too unhappy with this preliminary inventory, or with my initial classification, which was summary and primitive, to be sure, but which (like all the rest of my work) I considered as provisional. It therefore remained for me to actually tell the corresponding stories. To do that, I would have to undertake the massive task of organizing my materials. Clearly there was no question of unloading my narratives just any old way, like the table of contents in a collection of tales and legends. On the contrary, I would have to organize them in a coherent series: connecting, within a unified whole, all the characters proceeding from different worlds and making the adventure of each of them a symbolic stage in the unfolding of a story, thus repeating the procedure of the writers of the Jewish Bible or the Homeric epics, who had managed to weld together stories coming from diverse traditions and belonging to differing cycles. Only in that way could I succeed in making my readers feel the existence of a link continuing from generation to generation, like a breath passing down from the beginning to the end of a single family saga. I had to do all that while at the same time not smothering the cohort of my ancestors under the weight of the exotic, the picturesque, or worse yet, the heavy mantle of hagiography.

A difficult task, whose extravagance I vaguely sensed, and which seemed to me to require preliminary theoretical reflection (particularly on the notions of the epic and the ironic, based on two of my current idols, Thomas Mann and Lukács), which I did not wish to undertake immediately. It would be better, I told myself, after this expeditious and fruitful roundup, to try to go back to the little world, close at hand, of my family.

THE TWO ORPHANS

I am telling you about what was.
– Odilon Redon, *Journal*

With regard to the recent past, I knew what my main subject would be. It consisted of three characters. Three: the magical number already struck me as a good omen. Very quickly, as in the case of the patriarchs or Dumas's musketeers, I acquired the habit of designating these three by their first names alone: Jacob, Menahem, Mimoun. But they represented far more for me than the patriarchs or the musketeers of my childhood. Contaminated as I was (and more and more every year) by pagan thought, I saw these tutelary figures as a triad of divinities whose statues would share, with neither rivalry nor overlap, the vast temple of family memory, or perhaps as something like the waxen masks some Roman nobles placed in the atria of their residences and which they proudly displayed, to prove the antiquity of their family origins, in funeral processions.

But I had to bring these statues to life, resuscitate these masks. With them, I had to leave myth and finally enter into the concreteness of history. To be sure, I had never had an opportunity to see them, since all three had died before I was born; I therefore knew neither the sound of their voices nor their favorite postures, nor any of the little peculiarities that must have made each of them, to his entourage, a unique person. They were nevertheless the first of my lineage whose portraits were not produced through imagination alone. I knew with certainty these three faces, preserved in old sepia photographs – as big as postcards, they were about to fall out of the worn pages of the family album – which I had vainly tried to make speak.

This was enough to intimidate me: would I be able, with only my words, to sketch these emblematic characters in their very truth? Jacob, Menahem, Mimoun . . . did I even have the right to group them together like this? The bonds uniting them were clearly less simple than those linking their models in the Bible or in novels: they did not descend from father to son, like the patriarchs, and neither were they contemporaries or comrades in arms, like the musketeers. Hence it was difficult to take them all together, as a whole. To people other than myself, this triad might even seem arbitrary and artificially constituted. After all, I was the only one, along with my brothers and sisters, who could claim these three men at the same time: Menahem was our mother's father, Mimoun our father's father, and Jacob the father of our mother's mother. However, I could not keep from sensing, in the juxtaposition of these three singular destinies, something that went beyond the relationships of our family history alone. A sort of coherence that was important for me to demonstrate. Each of them had played out a role that he alone could play, but the diversity of these roles precisely represented, for the historical period involved, almost the whole spectrum of the possible. And this would permit me to make of them, in all good conscience (I was sure that I was betraying neither history nor legend) my principal heroes.

I still had to find the right way of approaching them. I knew from the outset that I would have to produce more than a simple, sober narrative of their deeds. I wanted to grasp them from within, to imagine the mental space they had lived in, to rediscover the way they saw themselves and their entourage. What were Jacob's thoughts when he married his daughter Esther to Menahem, his young, orphaned nephew? What were Menahem's fears and hopes when he decided to depart from Meknès, leaving behind his brother Mimoun? How did Jacob, Menahem, and Mimoun see their future, and that of their numerous children? This was a quest for which, given the lack of reliable sources – since family memory, more concerned with adding a flattering detail to the golden legend than with exploring in depth the personalities of its shining knights, was not of much help to me – I found myself repeatedly resorting to my own imagination as an amateur psychologist, bravely sounding the hearts and minds, as in the good old days when authors had the right to know everything (and the duty to tell everything) about the most delicate oscillations affecting their heroes' souls.

If I accepted this risk, it was because I was well aware that in compensation I would be able to make progress in another area: large-scale historical reconstitution. My three heroes would be assigned, in addition to their uncontested starring roles in my family epic, a genuine destiny on the level of Moroccan history. I grasped the scope of the literary benefit I could draw from this opening out onto the stage of history: the whiffs of exoticism that it would allow me to introduce would be a real boon.

If, for example, I took Jacob Ohana, it was clear that I had to center my whole work on his relationship with Moulay Hassan. That would take me into the very heart of the system of the Moroccan monarchy. In this way I could show the stages of its progressive decline: the exhausting battles against constantly renewed Berber opposition (nothing even prevented me from slipping in a few battles, with the deafening roar of cannon, headlong cavalry charges, and especially the smell of gunpowder, all of which are obligatory elements) and the tense diplomatic game that had to be played to fend off the awakening appetites of the European powers. But I could also dilate on the splendors of another age, which this monarchy was still able to maintain. I dreamed of a page, among many others, on the sumptuous ceremonies prepared for the arrival within the palace compound, one fine May morning, of a delegation from France (that of the Duc de Morny, for example): a page whose main feature would have been a description – in great detail, as in a big scene in a Hollywood movie, with the sunlight reflecting off shimmering headgear: cocked hats, kepis, shakos, or peaked caps – of the officers of the different regiments, all in dress uniforms, impeccably lined up at the moment at which, preceded by his green parasol, the sultan appeared on his magnificent white horse.

If I then turned to Menahem, I could enter with him, during the first years of the Protectorate, one of the great receptions held on the hill where the Residence stood, where, in the perfectly choreographed ballet of the guests arriving in little separate groups and crossing the brightly lit hall to greet Lyautey, the turbans, tarbooshes, fezzes, and immaculate djellabas of certain Moroccan high dignitaries captivated the eyes of the newly disembarked young French officers and their wives.

I therefore resolved to write many such pages, for my own intense pleasure (and, I hoped, that of my reader). But wisely putting off until later the composition of these bold pieces, I wanted first to do something more immediately useful: I undertook a sketch of the parallel lives of my two grandfathers, Menahem and Mimoun.

I was well aware that they would not immediately appear imposing; I had to extract the ore from the gangue. Fortunately, I quickly discovered that all I had to do, in order to raise them to the status of epic or novelistic characters, was to pay attention to the complicitous winks a friendly Providence seemed to have expressly set up for their future heir, who was in love with literature.

The first wink: the original family configuration, within which they were born and grew up. From the outset, I found myself in an atmosphere including these basic literary ingredients: love, death, adventure. Just imagine it.

At a date that no one could determine for me (sometime between 1840 and 1850), Yonah (also known as Jonas) Benabou (or Ben Abou), who followed, in Meknès, the currency exchanger's trade (which the proliferation of Moroccan and foreign currencies made indispensable), and his wife Jamila (whose family name I do not know, to my great regret) had a son, whom they named David. Young David, who became a businessman (though I cannot say what his business was), married Zahra Oliel, whose sister, Hannah, was the wife of Jacob Ohana, the millionaire (and this gives some indication of the family's social status). David and Zahra had two children: Menahem, in 1865, and Mimoun, in 1870. But shortly after Mimoun was born, Zahra suddenly died. Since she was still a young woman, her death surprised her family, and the midwife was suspected of having had something to do with it. However, they were not able to prove anything, and because there was no explanation, this unfortunate matter long remained a source of doubt, uneasiness, and injustice. Grief overwhelmed David, who was scarcely any older than his wife, and who loved her passionately. In fact, the young widower, who was sensitive and fragile, never succeeded in recovering from the loss of his beloved: he died, inconsolable, only a few months later.

This prologue, as sentimental and somber as the beginning of a popular serial, plunges Menahem and Mimoun into the very romantic condition of orphans. But in the midst of their misfortune, Providence does not forget them: they are taken in by their paternal grandparents, Yonah and Jamila. Concerning Yonah's role in this, I know nothing. He, too, probably died soon afterward, leaving behind him only a small nest egg. By all accounts, the central character in the story is Jamila. Energetic, resolute, intelligent, she immediately takes charge of the two orphans' destiny. Had she had other children, other grandchildren? On this subject, I have no certain knowledge (it seems that family curiosity didn't extend to collateral branches[1]). However that may be, Jamila saw to it that Menahem and Mimoun got a good education. The city's resources in this domain, although limited, were not negligible: Meknès had had, in the seventeenth and eighteenth centuries, a large number of rabbis, who were often exceptional teachers; the city, which had remained an important center for Torah studies, also had, back of some of the synagogues, a dozen yeshivot,[2] which offered the most traditional sort of teaching. It was in one of these study groups that the two orphans received their Hebrew education. But on Jamila's advice, they also studied classical Arabic – which Menahem, with a Muslim scholar as his tutor, learned quite well – and later on, French and Spanish.

They had hardly emerged from adolescence when they were separated from the woman who had served them as a mother. Approaching old age and believing she had done more than her duty, Jamila decided to satisfy her very old desire to go to the Holy Land. 'To die there,' she said. In spite of her grandsons' pleas, she refused to give up her plans. She was not the first in her family. Since the sixteenth century, a certain number of Moroccan rabbis had gone to live in Palestine, particularly in Safed, to study the Kabalah there. Among these was the Salomon Abou, whose synagogue, as we have seen, still stands in a charming little street named Rehov Abou. But since the middle of the nineteenth century, this movement had become more prominent,

1. We may nevertheless propose the following hypothesis: David was not Jamila's only child (a family with a single child was very rare at that time), but he was her only male child. If she had had another son, it would have been he, according to custom, who would have taken care of his orphaned nephews.

2. The plural of yeshiva, schools for Talmudic studies.

and the convoys henceforth headed toward Tabariya. In any case, the deepest wish of all pious Jews, in Morocco as in the rest of the world, was to be buried in Palestine, if possible in Jerusalem, on the Mount of Olives. A tiny number succeeded in being buried there; they were thus well-placed to be first in line on Resurrection Day. The others limited themselves to an alternative solution: they were buried along with small bags of precious Palestinian earth, which they had kept by them all their lives.

Still another windfall for me was being able to add to my literary project this choice bit: the itinerary taken from Meknès to Jerusalem by my valiant and very pious great-great-grandmother. I immediately plunged into a few of the countless *Journeys in the Orient* written by nineteenth-century travelers. I even began to write parts of 'A Grandmother's Travel Log,' in which Jamila, constantly thinking about her grandsons, was to note down – in the rather unpolished language I supposed her to have spoken (I knew nothing about her education) – her impressions as she went along. With enormous pleasure, I described the various stages of her journey, skipping over the inevitable dull moments and lingering over the intense ones. First of all, the wait: waiting, day after day, for the formation of a caravan that will take her from Meknès to Tangier (the very name of this city, with its promise of exoticism and mystery, obviously made me salivate). And then, one morning, the departure: under the protection of a large escort of armed horsemen (in fact, as a traveler of the time puts it, 'the system consists of taking brigands along with you in order to avoid meeting them on the road'), the caravan finally starts out, with its dozens of travelers, its camels, its replacement horses, its pack mules, its carefully rolled tents, its small army of footmen, camel drivers, mule drivers, and servants of all kinds, who are found in the evenings, once the animals have been hobbled, squatting around the campfires, singing.

The route is almost always the same (first they go west, down the valley of the Sebou; then north by way of Ksar-el-Kebir and Larache), but the journey is virtually endless (the daily stages are short, and every evening the camp has to be pitched, and everything packed up again in the morning) and full of unforeseeable incidents. In the absence of roads and bridges, they are constantly delayed, during the rainy season, by wet roads, flooding wadis (then they have to set up camp and wait for the water to go down), uncrossable fords (then they use, as in the time of Jugurtha's war, rafts made of inflated bladders connected by poles, and getting a whole caravan across can take days); and no matter what the season, they are always risking skirmishes with the tribes whose territory they are traversing. In Tangier, they have to wait again, until the departure of the next boat, which, taking its time, sails over the Mediterranean as far as the Egyptian coast. Thus they found themselves in Port Said, where they got off. There, once again, they waited for the formation of a caravan, which finally took them, by short stages, to the Holy City. Jamila thus endured the test of the interminable journey and arrived in Jerusalem, where she in fact spent her final years and where she was, in accord with her wish, buried.

Henceforth alone, the two brothers are obliged to take care of themselves. Although they are different in character (Mimoun, rather mischievous in his youth, remains energetic, even nervous; Menahem, on the contrary, playing the role of elder brother from the start, is calmer, more reflective, and gentler), the difficult conditions of their childhood have developed in them a deep feeling of solidarity and an affection that will last all their lives. This solidarity will not be useless. The society in which they have to make their way is a rigid one, with an archaic and largely undiversified economy. For centuries, people have been limiting themselves, as in the later Roman Empire, to their father's heritage. Where would an artisan or shopkeeper find the material means to break this indolent continuity, to repudiate the paternal model? But Menahem and Mimoun, because they are orphans, cannot be simply heirs. In order to survive, they have to create, innovate. An obligation they are able to take advantage of; it is imposed on them at a time when new outlets, unthinkable for earlier generations, are beginning to be offered to enterprising people. In a word, ambition, which up to that point could not arise – since it would only have led to ruin or frustration – finally becomes possible.

A new providential wink to the budding novelist: as in a good police investigation, I finally had my motive! Yes, the important word had been uttered: ambition. There it was, the passion that I was going to give to my two orphans to make them go a step further in their progress toward heroic stature. I therefore hastened to forge for them, on the basis of a few anecdotes, personalities suited to these premises: made for combat, full of enterprising spirit, capable, thanks to their courage and good sense, of being at ease in all situations. It remained only for me to follow them through their lives, which were at first closely connected, and then parallel. Starting, as is only right, with the eldest.

The first great turning point in Menahem's life is his marriage. At the beginning of the 1880s, he marries one of Jacob Ohana's daughters, Esther. A marriage that owes nothing to chance. The (very) young couple are second cousins (Esther's mother, Hanna Oliel, being, as we have already seen, the sister of Zahra Oliel, Menahem's mother); they thus knew each other very well and had been engaged. Hence this early union, arranged by the families in conformity with the most ancient customs, was warmly welcomed by its beneficiaries. I note in passing that a certain tendency to endogamy, originally made necessary by caste considerations (the difficulty of finding a spouse of the same social rank) or by the closeness of the relations among members of a given clan, will be maintained as a trademark among the following generations, those of my second cousins and even a little later, among a few distant cousins.

Was Jacob only acting out of generosity in taking an orphaned nephew under his wing, or, as a man of experience, had he divined the energy Menahem contained within him? A question that cannot be answered, but it would have pleased me very much, in the interest of the story's beauty, to be able to resolutely adopt the latter hypothesis! The perspicacious old millionaire, foreseeing a generation ahead of time the end of the old Morocco, giving his daughter to the young man who knows how to make a choice place for himself in the new order of things – that would have been a very beautiful symbol . . .

However that may be, Jacob Ohana's strong personality, as the leading figure of the Jewish community in Meknès, puts its stamp on Menahem. With the help of his father-in-law – who thus also plays, in a way, the role of the dead father – the young man will be able to get a start in business: with an associate, he opens a clothing shop. At the same time, he enters the life of the community, of which he will soon become the vice-president. In order to get supplies of cotton and wool fabrics, he is led to make trips to Tangier, the principal – indeed, the only – center of culture and economic activity, because of the port's regular relations with Christian Europe, and particularly with Spain and France. There, he establishes contact with a commercial firm run by an important merchant by the name of Toledano, an importer of flour, tea, and sugar. A very lucrative business: the importance of tea and sugar in the Moroccan diet is well known; still today they are considered necessities of the first rank. Menahem becomes the Toledano firm's representative for the Meknès area.

This will be the beginning of his fortune. After a few years, he is in a position to have his own house built, to restore Rabbi Schemaya's old synagogue, which had been abandoned, and to bring his brother Mimoun into his business.

But his commercial occupations are not enough to exhaust Menahem's energy. He is attracted by other activities. Open to Europe, aware of the fact that Morocco cannot long remain on the periphery, he prepares his children for the changes that he sees coming. He begins to have French and Spanish lessons given to David, the eldest of his sons (the very one who was later to introduce me to the joys of printing).

Here, another wink from Providence. Menahem's concern with pedagogy and language are richly rewarded. It happens that the professor in charge of teaching French to young David is a friend of the French consul in Rabat, Leriche, whom Menahem thus gets to know. The two men take to each other. Like many of his colleagues, such as the consul in Fez, Gaillard, or the one in Mogador, Jeannier (an unusual figure, a misanthropic esthete, who found the Arabic spoken in Morocco insufficiently pure, and prided himself on having taught his old parrot to speak a more perfect Arabic), the consul, Leriche, is a collector and a lover of the Arabic language. He finds in Menahem a conversation partner who shares his passion. They see each other often. Leriche is looking for a particularly rare manuscript which he wants to add to his collection, probably an illuminated Koran; Menahem succeeds in finding it and makes the consul a present of it. A genuine friendship develops. To the point that Leriche, at a juncture when France is seeking partners in Morocco, does not hesitate to offer Menahem the position of vice-consul. In order to make it possible for him to exercise his new functions, which require him to protect the interests of French nationals in his sector, he will be given the status of a French 'protegé,' which removes him from the jurisdiction of Moroccan courts and puts him under that of the French courts alone. This is the first step in the process of the official 'Frenchification' of the family. It pleased me to point out, for its picturesque value, that at exactly the same time an unfortunate teacher at the Alliance Israélite who, through an incredible series of blunders (due to his 'civilized' scorn for the 'barbarians' among whom he believed himself to have been assigned), had promptly used up the fund of goodwill from which he had benefited on arrival (and who also had his eye on the post of vice-consul) and was doing all he could in his reports to present Menahem as a dangerous enemy of education . . .

Menahem fulfilled his office with competence and enthusiasm, which led the local representatives of France to offer him additional functions: the postmaster in Tangier made him responsible for the French postal service in Meknès.[3] There, aided by his eldest son David and later by his nephew (who was going to be his son-in-law and was also named David; this was my father), Menahem ran the postal service for sixteen years, with the symbolic salary of one franc per year. A service whose importance I intended to stress: in the absence of a banking system, the postal service was responsible for transfers of funds between France and the French nationals in Morocco, a role it continued to play, moreover, during the first years of the Protectorate.

A hard worker whose efforts were appreciated, Menahem piles up positions: already vice-consul and postmaster, he also becomes president of the Jewish community, the manager of the Rabbinical school (the ancestor of the Talmud Torah where I was to have a very brief career), as well as a Jewish dispensary, be-

3. The lack of such a postal service in Morocco at that time had led the European powers to create their own postal services: thus there were French, English, and German postal services. To the great delight of certain contemporary philatelists.

nevolently directed by a French military doctor, who was his personal friend.

During this whole period, which precedes – and lays the groundwork for – the establishment of the Protectorate, Menahem shuttles back and forth between Meknès and Tangier, escorted by armed mercenaries, with tents and food supplies, to report to the French authorities concerning his activities. It is during one of these trips that is situated the episode, so often mentioned by my mother, of the German emperor's 'visit.'

But the good days in Meknès do not last. The city lives in fear of incursions by the Berber tribes in the surrounding area, particularly the Zemours, who are always ready to rebel against a steadily weakening central power. The first years of the new century are marked by serious disturbances that deeply shake the whole country: the disintegration of state authority accelerates. This is also the period of the young Sultan Moulay Abdel-Aziz's naive escapades. This adolescent wearing a crown (who, though he did not rise to the heights of a Caligula, seemed to me not to wholly deserve the scorn with which he was generally regarded) was getting bored on his throne; and so he constantly brought from Europe, at great expense, countless new objects to add to his wealth: velocipedes of all kinds, the latest gramophones, and – a surrealistic sight *avant la lettre* – a magnificent grand piano that an astonished French traveler was one day to find standing in the sun in a Laroche merchandise depot. It is also said (and I was only too glad to repeat it) that he quite often amuses himself by taking nude photographs of all the women in his harem, using a camera made of gold, and that he sometimes even sets off magnificent fireworks in full daylight on the immaculate terraces of his palace.

In Meknès, riots break out. The Jews are, as usual, the first to suffer, but in this case, they are not the only ones. The mellah has already been attacked once, in 1903. The prudent Menahem has recruited, for his protection, a small band of armed guards, which he places under the command of a fearsome old soldier, who answers to the name of Moha-ou-Izza and is not known for his loyalty. Spring 1911: a new siege. This time it lasts three months. Left without any public protection, and with Menahem's private guards ready to defect – since they would also like to share in the booty[4] – the residents of the neighborhood have to set up their own defense. Rifles and ammunition, which had been brought in secretly, are distributed to all ablebodied men, who take up positions at various points along the perimeter wall. Right in the middle of the Passover festival, the resistance is organized; the terrace of our family's house, which is the highest in the neighborhood, serves as an observation and command post. The attackers, surprised by a reaction they had not anticipated, end up withdrawing. To be sure, this was not the siege of Rome, nor the siege of Carthage, nor the siege of Jerusalem. But in the end the episode seemed to me to have a certain grandeur. It would be easy, I thought, to inflate it a bit, when the time came, and give it a worthy place in my epic.

After these events, Menahem takes a bold step, which will turn out to be decisive: he leaves Meknès. Is he discouraged by the continuing instability? Does he sense that there is no future

4. I owe to my eldest brother, who heard it from my father, a more precise version of this change. At the moment when the situation seemed hopeless, Moha-ou-Izza went to see Menahem and told him that since all the Jews' property was going to be taken anyway, it would be better to have this painful formality carried out – gently, and to their exclusive advantage – by his devoted guards, rather than by the violent mob of attackers . . . we know that this kind of reasoning (why let others commit crimes that one can commit oneself?) was to have a singular currency among certain French leaders under the Occupation.

in Moulay Ismael's old capital stripped of its ancient glory and that he has to have the courage to turn his back on that past? Probably. I would be tempted to add (for the pure pleasure of its romantic character, since none of my sources mentions this) a more personal motivation. Perhaps this departure is for him a way of showing that he can now operate on his own by detaching himself from the tutelage – or at least from the sphere of influence – of his father-in-law's family. Menahem chooses to settle in Tangier, a city whose many advantages he already knows. But he will not stay there long. In the meantime, his children have grown up. His eldest son, David, has reached the age to marry. A wife is found for him in Rabat: her name is Rachel Benattar, and her father is the consular agent for seven nations, including the Austro-Hungarian Empire ('seven flags flew over the door of my house,' she proudly declared, but I never dared ask her whether she was just speaking metaphorically).

Rabat is beginning to develop, and Menahem realizes it is where the future is. He takes up residence there. His wealth grows and his responsibilities as well. Once the government of the Protectorate is set up, he is one of the people whom the French authorities trust and whom they involve in their projects. New, useful friendships are established. Menahem is encouraged to open a foreign currency exchange at a time when the circulation of money is becoming increasingly intense.

Paralleling this economic expansion, a new, more ambitious social life is being organized under Lyautey's powerful influence. People get used to going for an evening walk along the oceanfront, under the pergolas of the Oudayas garden, amid the bougainvilleas. On the hill of the Residence, from which there is an incomparable view, balls, theatrical productions, and concerts become increasingly numerous (my mother still remembered with wonder a production of Mascagni's *Cavalleria rusti-*

cana,[5] to which she had been invited). These festivities will not be interrupted and will become even more conspicuously insouciant during the Great War, because Lyautey wants to give everyone the impression that France's power is in no way affected by the battles going on in faraway Europe. Menahem's youngest daughters, who are now receiving, like their brothers, a European education, navigate with ease among the French officers – young and dashing, as they should be – who at the same time discover the grandeur of their mission (to fulfill France's 'imperial vocation' in this old kingdom that has finally emerged from its torpor) and its pleasures (dancing a waltz with the dark-skinned heiresses of the local Jewish notables).

Menahem and Esther's marriage had been very fruitful: four sons and seven daughters filled their house. A house that, alongside rooms in the traditional style, with chests, divans, and carpets, is also now decorated with European furniture that formerly belonged to the Spanish consul. Over this little world Esther reigns. Her husband's status and the number and quality of her 'relations' require that she live in a ceremonious manner whose obligations she assumes gracefully, knowing how to create around herself, in the coming and going of visitors and guests from various origins, a permanent atmosphere of playful diversion. I cannot help thinking that in so doing she was trying to reproduce, adapting it to the new age, her parents' way of life in Jacob Ohana's big house in Meknès. From one generation to the next, there is – according to the stories – the same cordiality, the same sense of welcome, but also the same taste for decorum. And when my mother, speaking of Esther, told me that she was 'always covered with jewelry and dressed like an idol,' I could not help comparing these words with those Loti used in describ-

5. A lyrical drama produced in French translation at the Opéra Comique from 1902 on.

ing Hannah, Esther's mother: 'She is the most sumptuous of all the women, with her scarlet velvet skirt, her blue velvet blouse disappearing under the gold embroidery, and her earrings interwoven with tiny pearls and emeralds as big as walnuts.'

Menahem thinks the time has come to take on French nationality. Marshal Lyautey advises against doing so: 'This naturalization, which you amply deserve because of the eminent service you have rendered to France, can only cause disturbances in your family, since your sons will have to go to France to do their military duty. Besides, it will afford you no additional guarantee, because you already enjoy, along with your family, French protection, which confers on you the rights of citizenship without the burdens connected with it.'[6] But a few years later, when the system of 'protections' came to an end, Menahem and all his family became French. This had required that the French government take a rather unusual diplomatic step: obtaining, in conformity with the Madrid convention of 1880, the severance of the so-called ties of 'perpetual allegiance' that normally connected Moroccan subjects to the Crown. This explains the presence, among the family papers carefully preserved in my father's cabinet, of a document acknowledging the Sultan's consent to this severance (transmitted to the general Residence through the grand vizier, Mohammed el Mokri). As a French citizen, Menaham will gain access to lands reserved for colonization: he acquires in this way several dozen hectares of vineyards,[7] which provide a landed basis – perceived as the final stage of social success – for an already considerable patrimony.

6. I don't know who now has the original of this letter, from which my uncle Georges copied out this extract for me.

7. The grapes from which my elder brother, while he was still a child, sold to earn pocket money.

For the man who henceforth appears as a wealthy patriarch (and here the heir-narrator felt a great desire to adopt a quasi-biblical tone, like that in Hugo's poem 'Booz endormi'), it is the most brilliant period, unanimously elevated by family memory, moreover, to the rank of a golden age: his fortune firmly based on diverse activities, the privileged status of French citizenship, relationships and friends in the new governing circles, official recognition obtained through the granting of two decorations, the (Moroccan) Ouissam Alaouite, and the (Tunisian) Nicham Iftikar. What I called 'the affair of the avenging safe' even provides an event that attests, in a public manner, that the family benefits from Providence's special protection. Here are the facts: Menahem's house being constantly guarded, and therefore a difficult target for burglars, two would-be thieves, very inventive and using the most advanced methods of the time (which were still pretty rudimentary), developed the following strategy: they would dig, starting from the cellar of a neighboring house, a tunnel that was to bring them right under the room with the safe, which was supposed to be full of treasures (including some very beautiful jewels recently bought from a Brazilian businessman). After several hours' work, our two thieves had almost reached their goal. Only a thin layer of dirt separated them from the coveted loot. But their technical competence, particularly with regard to timbering (a very difficult art, as anyone who builds tunnels knows) was not equal to their powers of invention: some error in calculation must have slipped into their estimate of the massive safe's weight. This allowed immanent justice to act in a very exemplary fashion. The safe suddenly fell through the floor, which had become too weak, and crushed one of the thieves, who remained there, howling and unable to move. The other thief, who had tried to get away, leaving his unfortunate, half-buried associate to his fate, was immediately caught by the guards. The story obviously got all around the city, and for a long time it discouraged all sorts of crooks from acting on their larcenous desires. Menahem thus did not lose his magnificent jewels, which were later to be handed down to his two youngest daughters.[8]

This blessed period was incarnated, in my view, by the famous apartment house in Rabat. A modern building with several stories, built on a highly symbolic site (in the immediate neighborhood of the well-named Rue des Consuls, at the junction point between the mellah, the medina, and the European city, and not far from the Alliance Israélite school), it seemed to me to materialize the twin ambition that had driven Menahem: giving the family a residential base worthy of its influence and making it a meeting point for all the different cultures that took part in the new Morocco.

But history, like the novel, does not like to linger over these moments of happiness. I was later to see this ceremonious period brusquely interrupted. The reason? The aftershocks – which came late to Morocco – of the Great Depression of 1929. At the beginning of the 1930s, Menahem, weakened by illness, has left most of the responsibility for his affairs to his son David. The latter, as was usual among leading families in the community, has agreed to help a large number of small merchants and artisans in the Jewish community by giving them his guarantee at the banks. The general decline of the economy and the bankruptcy of commerce strike with their full force the businesses in which most of Menahem's fortune is invested. The result is disaster. Unanticipated, unjust, irreparable. The vineyards, the pride of the family, have to be sold, and the other property is

---

8. The later fate of these jewels was less picturesque: some of them disappeared, no doubt stolen by an unscrupulous maid; the rest were sold to finance the purchase of a fabric shop which was, for many decades, the realm of my youngest aunt.

confiscated. Every time my mother mentioned this confiscation tears came to her eyes, and my family always remembered it as a traumatic event. I resolved to accentuate its dramatic character, and I had already reread for this purpose the appropriate pages of Balzac's *La Muse du département* and Flaubert's *Madame Bovary* (I had never had an opportunity to see *La Traviata*). I managed to slightly attenuate the sadness of this episode by recalling the successful efforts to save, from the patrimony about to be swallowed up, a few rare objects (porcelain, silverware) that quickly took on the status of relics.

Not long afterward, another painful blow was to strike the unfortunate patriarch: the death of his wife. This was the last of his misfortunes, for just as his father, the overly sensitive David, had not long survived Zahra, Menahem did not long survive Esther. He passed away early in 1939. I was to be born a few months later, which explains why I was given his name as my Hebrew forename.

Why is it that I cannot mention my grandfather Mimoun without immediately thinking of his grave? I don't know. The memory, no doubt very old, which must lie at the origin of this automatic reflex (which has persisted from my childhood up to this day) had apparently already become blurred at the time when, seeking materials for my family epic, I began to ask myself this kind of question. In spite of my later efforts, I have never succeeded in reconstructing it with a reasonable degree of certainty. If I am now making a further attempt (whereas I could simply take it as a simple given, and say: 'that's the way it is,' and go on), it is to set my mind at ease, so that it cannot be said that I have refused to explore something that bothers me. I have finally arrived at a rather simple hypothesis. I believe that I must have discovered, at precisely the same moment, both the existence *and* the grave of this personage who died fifteen years before I was born, who was more or less absent from my mother's stories, and who must have been unknown to me up to that time. But when, and especially with whom, did I make this double, conjoint discovery? Was it my father, who may have sometimes taken me along on his visits to the cemetery? I find this difficult to believe, since I don't remember, during the whole period of my early childhood, going anywhere with my father other than to the synagogue; in addition, I don't think filial piety would have been likely to take, in a man as reserved and discreet as my father, the rather ostentatious form of visits to the grave, which seems to me (but I may be wrong about this) rather to be, like certain half-magical and half-religious practices, the sort of thing women did. My mother, then? If that were the case, why would I have forgotten it, whereas so many things she said or did that were far less important have remained in my memory? I concluded from this, fairly logically, that it is my aunt Zahra, my father's eldest sister, who is at the root of my first contacts with Mimoun and his burial place. For two decisive reasons: she alone had remained sufficiently attached to old traditions to go regularly to pray, at certain times of year, at her father's grave; and she alone had enough authority for my mother to allow her to take me on such a visit. The more I think about it, the more plausible this hypothesis seems. Perhaps it was also because of my aunt's calming influence that these contacts with the idea and the reality of death, which were new to me, did not disturb me. To the point that for a whole period (I was then eight or nine years old, and we were still living in the Rue du Dispensaire), I sometimes went on my own to spend a few moments in the nearby cemetery.

A cemetery that was not without its attractions. The long, ochre-colored wall that surrounded it was immediately adjacent to the neighborhood, from which it was separated only by the width of a single street. The thick foliage of trees and tall grasses that grew freely in it had made the whole area along this wall a very special place. Deserted during the day, at nightfall it became a meeting place for impatient teenaged couples who, unable to go anywhere else because of the extraordinary ambient puritanism, found it the only possible place to indulge in furtive kissing and necking. Some neighborhood kids even found it amusing to go there, as soon as it grew dark, to prowl around the thickest bushes, singing loudly (I remember the first words of their song: 'Lovers are unhappy'), in the hope of finding couples hiding in them, who would be cruelly interrupted right in the middle of their amorous activities. The cemetery itself, on the other side of the wall, was in an open area of wheatfields and olive orchards. Since the construction of the new mellah, it had finally replaced the old necropolis, tiny and overpopulated, where, for almost three centuries, cadavers had been piled up in successive layers (I hope future archaeologists enjoy their attempts to determine the tormented stratigraphy of this narrow piece of earth).

The cemetery gate was always open. I sometimes went to visit my grandfather, especially around Hillulah (toward the end of spring, between Passover and Pentecost), which was also the time of the great pilgrimages to the tombs of the saints. Flowers were then appearing all over the cemetery. Not the ones the living brought to their dead. This custom, which is eminently pagan, was unknown; instead, both Jews and Muslims customarily placed a simple stone on the edge of the grave. The cemetery's flowers were living flowers: they grew spontaneously in the large vacant spaces near the entrance, but quite far from the area where the graves were. They sprang up everywhere, daisies and poppies by the thousands, massed together on their long stems in flowerbeds with a wild sort of harmony, and the slightest breeze made them undulate.

I went in, looking apprehensively at a few graves that were clearly isolated, along the wall, on my right. They were very different from the rest: neither a marble headstone nor an engraved inscription, only a simple, anonymous, whitewashed construction that no one ever visited. I had been told that they were the graves of people who had been banished from the community, for some serious infraction of Mosaic law. I remembered, however, that in the old cemetery, it was on the contrary those who were the pride of the community that had a right to the plots nearest the wall.

Under the hot sun, I hurriedly traversed, trampling a few weeds, the long distance that separated me from the part of the cemetery where the graves were lined up in the strict order proper to cemeteries. They were almost all alike in their simplicity: a raised tomb topped by a sheet of gray or white marble. There was as yet nothing resembling the large family tombs or monuments that elsewhere pretentiously perpetuate the memory of local notables. For this pious community, equality in death was not merely a theme for Saturday afternoon sermons.

I found without difficulty my grandfather's grave, the third one in the third row. The white marble, on which an epitaph had been carefully engraved in both Hebrew and French, felt pleasantly cool to my lips and my forehead, when I bent down to kiss it, murmuring the appropriate benediction. When I got up, my head was empty. No precise thought. Not even an emotion. Except the one caused by the approach of two or three of the enormous beautifully colored butterflies – which flew so slowly that they were easy to catch – that constantly flew over the flowers and sometimes drifted toward the graves. I probably didn't really know what the words 'meditate' or 'reflect' meant, and perhaps I hadn't even encountered them yet. So to give my reverie a content, I read and reread the double epitaph; then I tried to reconstitute, in my sluggish memory, some of the features I had noted in the single photo of my grandfather, comparing them with those of my father. I easily recalled the long, distinguished face, the broad, prominent forehead, the very bright eyes (which my father had inherited, and after him my sister Marie), the almost too-refined mouth almost completely covered by a large, white mustache (my father's salt-and-pepper mustache was more discreet). But no matter how hard I tried, I couldn't put everything together. Some element was always missing, and the image remained blurred. Mimoun's face still presents itself to me in this way, connected with these moments of slight intellectual languor, in a context whose rather magical serenity struck me far more than its funerary character.

Undeniably, I knew Mimoun less well than Menahem. My mother's stories, which were my chief source, did not give the two brothers equal attention. And this was no accident. First of all, my mother had been, as is only natural, less close to her uncle than to her father. And then, by not mentioning Mimoun, she manifested – unconsciously, of course – her sulky reserve with regard to an uncle who had rather too promptly become her father-in-law.

My father, who was clearly in a better position to provide me with the complementary information I needed, ultimately did not do so. Not that he ever refused to answer my questions. On the contrary. But that was just it: I had to ask him questions, and I was not always able to do that. He lacked both the feeling and the inclination for long stories told over and over again, in which one gets lost and to which one always returns, each time adding new ornaments to them. Meticulous and concise, he could without hesitation come up with a name, give a precise date, report verbatim what someone said (if my mother loved sayings and proverbs, he loved quotations); but except for a few exceptional moments, you couldn't rely on him to characterize someone, to describe a setting, to render an atmosphere. Only my eldest brother succeeded, on certain evenings, in making him emerge from his reserve.

This usually occurred at the end of our long Passover dinners. The mood suddenly became relaxed. Laughing, we had drunk – leaning, as we were supposed to do, on our left elbows – the last of the four ritual cups of wine. We had gone through the whole cycle of prayers and songs, including the one I particularly loved ('A kid, a kid, which my father bought for two coins'), which was sung only in Arabic, everyone chiming in on the refrain. The nephews, sweetly snuffling in their mothers' arms, had long since fallen asleep. My father, now released from all the religious tasks with which he had been busy ever since sunup, and happy, now felt available. At a word or an allusion made by my elder brother, he became animated. His memory got carried away. He liked to talk about his childhood and adolescence, and very quickly, he moved on to memories of the most difficult times. His remarks evoked a universe as yet unknown to me: characters, events, rites that my mother had not up to that point thought it wise to tell me about.

There was the story of the Jewish matron (I've forgotten her name) whose house had been pillaged during a Berber attack: she had climbed up on one of the columns of Bab el Mansour – the monumental gate in the heart of the old city – and did not hesitate, when the sultan passed by on horseback in the midst of his black guard, to call out to him and publicly demand justice. And there was the story of the worthy Mordecai Loubaton, who had courageously gone, in April 1903, into the rebel camp to try to persuade their leader, the dreaded Bou Hamara ('the man with the she-ass') not to attack the mellah. There was also the story of shooting from the terrace of our house when the

Berber assailants were hacking away at the wall of the mellah, during the long siege of 1911. Or the one about the three bulls (white bulls, I think) that the Jews led out in a procession and sacrificed during Sultan Moulay Youssef's visit in 1923 in order to win his favor. I therefore had to be satisfied with a few stories told at these privileged moments and forego asking him myself directly; I went about this so badly that I soon exhausted my questions and his patience.

This relative lack of oral sources concerning Mimoun did not, however, seem to me a very serious matter. For the image of him I wanted to render, I could get along without the expedient amateur biographers – and even a few professionals – usually enjoy: the existence of a cloud of anecdotes floating around a name. Just as the figure of Menahem had been illumined by reference to that of Jacob, so the figure of Mimoun would take on meaning in relation to that of Menahem. In my two pairs of ancestors, I saw the same schema at work: a phase of close collaboration and family association, followed by a phase of separation, of going their separate ways. What interested me was following Mimoun along the path that had made him different.

One observation seemed to me inevitable: whereas Menahem moved around a great deal, went off in different directions, Mimoun remained attached to the city where he was born, Meknès, as if the younger brother's ambition was of another type – less personal, more communitarian – than his elder sibling's. It is true that there was a great deal to be done to improve life in the community of which Mimoun was to become, after his brother left, president. To the classic problems of administration were added specific difficulties connected with the period of transformation through which the Jews were living. In Mimoun, the debate between those who wanted to remain faithful to an essentially religious past and those who wanted to move toward a more secular future was transformed into an internal conflict. He resolved it – and for me this constituted his originality – by adopting, for himself as well as for those under his administration, an attitude that was apparently less audacious, and slightly more reticent, in comparison with his elder brother's innovative fervor. In my view, this prudence was embodied in an unusual bit of city planning: the creation of the neighborhood called 'the new mellah.'

The conditions under which Jews lived within the mellah, as it existed before the Protectorate, had become particularly unbearable. The neighborhood was still enclosed within very narrow limits, which had not budged since the reign of Moulay Ismail, a contemporary of Louis XIV. It was surrounded by crenelated walls, with entry through a single monumental gate that was closed at nightfall (it still existed when I was a child, but by then it was only a place to walk to on Saturday nights). In Mimoun's time, no new construction was authorized. Families were forced to live piled on top of one another, with the generations all mixed up, in the existing houses. The overpopulation, promiscuity, and deplorable hygienic conditions struck every visitor to the mellah, and I could not read some of their descriptions without deep uneasiness (which reminded me of the uneasiness aroused by my early readings on Nazi persecution). Tirelessly, the Jews requested permission to enlarge their neighborhood, without obtaining any more than promises that were never kept. The beginnings of the Protectorate did not much improve matters. When he inherits this situation, Mimoun first tries to deal with the most pressing issue, hygiene: he arranges, for the first time, regularly scheduled garbage pickup. Then he goes once again to argue the Jews' case before the French authorities. The latter are finally moved. Perpetuating a situation that had been going on for three centuries is unjust and absurd; moreover – a decisive argument – doing so constitutes a threat to public health. The problem is studied. A solution is proposed: open a new area for the Jews, near the neighborhoods reserved for Europeans, that is, in the upper city, the new city, about three kilometers from the mellah. The initial plans are drawn up, and seem extremely attractive. Everything is in conformity with the most advanced standards of colonial urban planning: broad, rectilinear streets, public streetlights, schools, parks, sewers. In addition, the financial conditions are enticing. However, this project does not win the expected approval. The community leaders, swayed by Mimoun, hesitate, hedge, worry. And end up saying no. No to what seemed an unhoped-for boon, but which they come close to seeing as a poisoned gift.

Mimoun is conscious of the significance of the turning point that this sudden move would constitute and dreads the foreseeable consequences. He knows that the secret of the community's survival has resided, for centuries, in its obstinate fidelity to its familial and religious structures: they have served as a fortress against the hazards of the outside world. Leaving the mellah, the heart of Jewish life, would not be merely a move, but a genuine migration. By coming closer to European society and its seductions, they would be opening themselves up to two great dangers. The first, which is very clear, is the decrease, and among some people the pure and simple abandonment, of religious observance (the example of other cities, where this process was already at work, provided some basis for Mimoun's fears). It is in fact difficult to remain faithful to the daily rituals, except in a context which makes it easy to carry them out: in the mellah, because of the collective pressure – which is continually exercised – transgression is practically impossible. The second danger is more insidious because it takes longer to appear: the rupture, the disintegration of the indispensable community bond and the values on which it is founded: the warmth and solidarity of the group. Perhaps Mimoun already anticipated the uneasiness that would characterize the 1950s, when a generation that had staked a great deal on 'Europeanization' and was beginning to encounter the latter's limits tried to return to its old values and discovered that they had, in the meantime, gone irreversibly to tatters.

The new neighborhood, with all the planned conveniences, would thus be built, not at the place initially proposed, but elsewhere, in the immediate vicinity of the mellah. More precisely: on the other side of the famous gate that formerly marked the boundary, and which was henceforth only a grandiose witness to a past that was anything but grandiose. This gave rise to the situation peculiar to Meknès, which juxtaposed two very different Jewish neighborhoods, the old mellah and the new. The old mellah was rather quickly left behind by all those who, having more or less integrated themselves into the economic networks set up by the Protectorate, had enough money to have a new house built for themselves in the new mellah. Only the poorest families and those that remained least open to the new order of things remained in the old mellah: minor artisans (tailors, cobblers, bookbinders) and small merchants with very few wares. Mimoun himself did not have time to move into the new neighborhood he had fathered: in 1924, during a trip to Rabat (which he had undertaken in order to formally invite Menahem and his family to his daughter's marriage), he contracted malaria and died from it; he was only fifty-three years old. The new mellah proceeded nonetheless. It developed and gradually took on the appearance of a 'small Jerusalem' – an unexpected mixture of modern city planning and ancient piety – that was so much to strike European visitors.

Thus, thanks to its president's circumspection, the Jewish community in Meknès experienced a development that was more harmonious (no rupture with the past) but undeniably slower than elsewhere. I discovered this with surprise as soon as I had a chance, during the first great family festivals after the war, to enter into contact with children of my age from other cities, and especially from the coastal cities. In their view, people from Meknès seemed to be 'behind the times.' Because we were still living almost exclusively among ourselves. Because we were still, in our daily activity, respectful of traditions and religious scruples they knew nothing about, or which, openly and without fear, they dared to mock. I remember that when I was ten, some of my cousins from Rabat, with whom I was spending part of the summer, understood hardly any Arabic and still less Hebrew, never went to the synagogue, lived in apartment buildings where their playmates were the children of Spanish or Portuguese neighbors, knew words (generally in close connection with the various organic functions localized in the area of the lower abdomen, concerning which their knowledge was limitless) I had never before heard spoken or read in any of my books, and, whereas I persisted with very reprehensible stubbornness in laboriously rolling my *r*'s, they possessed an impeccable 'Moroccan French' accent that allowed them to go everywhere without being noticed. All this obviously gave them, with respect to the rather oafish cousin I seemed to them to be, an intense feeling of superiority, which even their sense of family (which was in any case quickly eroding) did not succeed in making them conceal. I didn't know how to react. I could have wrapped myself nobly in the mantle of my still intense piety, called them assimilated Jews, or even *aphicoros,* for I had just learned, from one of my friends who was a rabbi's son, this expression which was considered the worst possible insult (I later discovered with amusement that it derived from the name of Epicurus and was primarily used, as it was among the ancient Romans, to vilify atheists). But secretly undermined by my profane readings, I was already no longer sufficiently sure that I was right. And I believe that had I been better informed, at that time, about the role played by my grandfather in the recent history of our city, I would have reproached him for having subjected me, through his excessive prudence, to such a damaging cultural lag.

INTERMITTENCIES

*The difficulty of this book
consists in the transitions,
and in making a whole out
of many different things.*
– Gustave Flaubert, letter
to L. Colet, 3 April 1852

*My poets were Larousse,
Chaix, Joanne, Vidal de la Blache.*
– Jean Cocteau, *Le Potomak*

Pages followed pages, but in a rather scattered way. Sometimes, I have to admit, in the greatest disorder. Not having succeeded, despite long months of effort, in finding a satisfying model for my work, I had decided, in order to avoid paralysis, to leave hanging, as long as I needed to, structural problems. And I had finally limited myself to starting three large dossiers, distinguished from each other by the color of their folders: 'Characters' (pale green), 'Objects' (light gray), and 'Instants' (salmon pink); these served, day by day, as the receptacle for all the fragments I could not fit into the various chapters already outlined. Depending on the moment, I spent my time fattening, by means of new additions, one or the other of my three initial dossiers, without following any rule other than my inclination. The latter, governed by successive, unpredictable enthusiasms, which were also of varying duration, was extremely variable and could lead me in the most diverse directions.

Thus it happened that one day, marveling at the discovery, in a bookseller's green box, of Sei Shônagon's *Pillow Book*, which made such original, and, in my view at least, such moving use of enumerations (I particularly liked certain optimistic series such as 'Things that make us happy,' 'Things that awaken a sweet memory from the past,' 'Occasions on which trivial things assume importance,' 'The most beautiful things in the world,' but I was also attracted to others that were more melancholy, such as 'Frightening things,' 'Embarrassing things,' and 'Things without grace'), that I decided I should also set out to construct lists.

I first attempted to recapitulate some of the objects in my parents' house that had once intrigued me, or – because they constituted the last concrete evidence of the family's glory – had long led me to daydream: the majestic copper samovar, which I had so much loved to see smoking on the day one of my brothers got married; the big Chinese porcelain plates, delicately decorated with flowers, foliage, and birds, that adorned the walls of the small blue living room; the silver knife rests, in the form of recumbent animals, which never came out of the cabinet except when they were polished and put on the table at the same time as the embroidered tablecloth and the big white napkins on festival evenings; the old, somewhat rusty saber, carelessly wrapped in a grayish cloth, which, when slipped beneath the bed of a young woman giving birth to a child, was supposed to provide magical protection against the attack of evil; a whole set of copper utensils that were never used, such as the incense burners and perfume burners in perforated copper that were taken out on rare occasions or the flagons with a small, rounded belly and a long, narrow neck that were filled with orange blossom essence to sprinkle on guests on certain occasions. Encouraged by the results of this first inventory, I immediately tried to list the few pleasant smells (through a sort of prudishness, I omitted the other kind) that had marked me: the smell of the oven, on Friday afternoons, when I went with the maid to get the round loaves my mother had herself kneaded for the Sabbath meals; the bitter-almond smell of the little jars of white glue that I used during so-called manual arts sessions; the smell of *dafina* (a favorite dish served at lunch on Saturdays), at the moment when my mother lifted the kettle lid to see if it was cooking properly; the perfume of coriander, which every evening began to saturate the kitchen as I nibbled, along with my youngest sister Esther, on a snack of bread and chocolate. But when I then tried to extend my classifying frenzy to other objects (successively: the sounds of the street and the house at different times of day and night; the names of my classmates, year by year, at the Alliance Israélite school; the addresses of all my uncles, aunts, and cousins in Rabat; the ritual foods at noon and evening meals on festival days, etc.), the result did not always give me all the satisfaction I expected, and I preferred to abandon, provisionally, this particular vein.

Another day (several weeks after having sketched out the pages on Menahem and Mimoun), driven by a kind of remorse, I felt it urgent to finally write my aunt Zahra's story: she had been waiting only too long to make her entry into the family literary pantheon, my dear old aunt, whose noble countenance came up every time I needed to give an example of self-abnegation and devotion. But, I thought, her story is much too beautiful to be disposed of in a few dry lines; here, in order to rise to the level of my subject, I had to match the innocence and simplicity of certain verses in Genesis or in the Book of Job. Or, failing that, I had to rediscover the religiously lyrical or elegiac inspiration of the ancient masters of Judeo-Moroccan poetry who had flourished in the seventeenth and eighteenth centuries (whom I had learned about in the course of my readings), such as Jacob, Moses, and Shalom, the three greats of the Abensour family, or else David Hassine. To be sure, they were not afraid of taking on literary tasks that were tough, to say the least, in matters of didactic poetry. One of them – Shalom, the last of the Abensours – had boldly versified the Hebraic calendar. Another, the prolific and malicious David Hassine (my favorite, because he was from Meknès), had gone even further: among other productions, he had undertaken to put into verse the rather austere rules governing the ritual slaughter of animals . . . such prestigious models could not but stimulate my natural penchant for pastiches and stylistic exercises. Thus I summoned the courage to launch into a transcription, in a hodgepodge, pseudo-biblical manner, of my aunt's story. The result was approximately (approximately because, not having been able to find a complete original version among my papers, I've had to reconstruct this text partly from memory) the following:

ZAHRA'S STORY

May every creature's mouth praise God's Name. Amen.

In the city called Mequinez, Joseph, son of Raphael, married Zahra, daughter of Mimoun, son of David, son of Yonah.

They lived five years in great harmony, but at the end of the fifth year, sorrow began to gnaw their hearts, for God had closed Zahra's womb, and she had had no children.

And Zahra knew that Joseph was sorrowing. And Joseph knew that Zahra was sorrowing.

One day, Zahra said to Joseph:

'Lo, God has refused to bless my womb, and I have not given you any children.

'But you cannot remain without an heir to bear your name, a son who will pray for you on the day of your death.

'So I will choose another woman for you, a second wife, I will care for her in my house and she shall be as a daughter to me.

'And God in his mercy will perhaps give her the children he has not given me.'

And Joseph said to Zahra:

'Zahra, Zahra, since God has put this plan in your heart, and these words in your mouth, I will not oppose them and I will put no obstacle in your way; it shall be as you wish.'

And Zahra chose and Zahra found, among the women in the city, a young virgin named Simha, daughter of Eleazar. Her family was not well known in the city, but her reputation was unstained and her heart was innocent of wickedness.

And Zahra went to Simha and said to her:

'Simha, lo, God has not allowed me to give Joseph, my husband, a child to bear his name, a son who will pray for him on the day of his death. Now, if you accept him, come with me, and you shall be Joseph's wife.

'I shall care for you in my house as my daughter, and God in his mercy will perhaps give you the children he has not given me.'

And Simha rejoiced in Zahra's words, and said to her:

'Zahra, Zahra, since God has put this plan in your heart, and these words in your mouth, I will not oppose them and I will put no obstacle in your way.

'If this is what you wish and desire, then I shall come with you to your house, and Joseph your husband shall be my husband.'

And Simha came to the house of Zahra and Joseph, and Joseph was her husband. And God in his mercy blessed Simha's womb.

And Simha bore a son and Simha bore two daughters. And Joseph and Zahra cared for Simha in every way.

And lo, in the dire month of Ab a cruel illness came to smite the city; and the people of the city died in great number. And Simha fell sick with this cruel illness. And God called the young Simha back to Him.

Joseph and Zahra sorrowed and wept, for Simha was for them as a dearly beloved daughter.

Half a year passed, and lo, the illness once again smote the city. And God called back to Him his servant Joseph. And Zahra wept for her husband Joseph, for he was loving and kind.

And Zahra turned toward the children of Joseph and Simha. And from that day onward, they were for her as her own children; and they always called her mother, for they had but little known their mother Simha.

And lo, it happened that one of the children, Raphael, went up into the land of Israel and prospered there.

And when Zahra grew old, Raphael sent a message to Zahra and said to her:

'Mother, now that you are old, and your daughters have grown into women, they no longer need your help. Come then into my house, the house of your son, in the land of Israel. In that way you shall know the children of your son who were born in the land of Israel. And you shall remain in the house of your son so long as God wills it.'

And Zahra answered Raphael:

'My son, if God wishes it, it shall be so, for your happiness and for mine.'

And Zahra summoned her two daughters and said to them:

'Lo, now I am old and my daughters are grown into women; they no longer need my help. Now I wish to go into the house of my son, in the land of Israel.

'And I shall know the children of my son who were born in the land of Israel. And I shall remain in the house of my son so long as God wills it.'

And Zahra's daughters answered:

'Mother, since you desire it and since you wish it, let it be so. As for us, we shall remain near the grave of Joseph our father, in order that his memory be blessed. But when our hearts shall cry out to see the face of our mother, then we shall go up to see her in the land of Israel.'

And Zahra went up into the land of Israel. She went into the house of her son and knew the children of her son who had been born in the land of Israel.

And every year, the daughters of Zahra went up into the land of Israel with their children, to see the face of Zahra their mother, and to rejoice with Raphael, their brother.

And Zahra thanked God, who allowed her to see her children and her children's children, every year.

And Zahra remained for five years in the house of her son.

And lo: at the end of the five years, God called his servant Zahra back to him.

Then the children of Zahra gathered in the house of Raphael, in the land of Israel; and for seven days and seven nights the house was full of their tears and the tears of their children.

And when they had wept many tears and were weary with mourning, they said:

'God gave us a father and a mother, and God has taken them away from us. But God, in His mercy, has not left us alone; he has sent us a second mother.

'She has lived with us as a good and righteous mother. And lo, now as a good and righteous mother, she rests near us, in the land of Israel.

'Praised be God, who gives and who takes away as He will.'

So ends the story of Zahra.

May every creature's mouth praise God's Name. Amen.

Since I was involved with biblical figures (or at least they seemed Biblical to me), I decided to stay with them a little longer. Hence I went immediately on to discuss the figures to whom I had given the name 'Guardians of the Flock,' the two great rabbis who had taken it upon themselves to keep their community on the right path. Two complementary and symmetrical figures: it was tempting to see in them the local reincarnation of the ancient antagonism – perpetually renewed – that had brought into confrontation, ever since the first century, the gentle Hillel and the surly Shammai. There was also a division of labor between our two tutelary rabbis. To me, this was apparent in the way each of them was brought into the Sabbath ceremony.

Rabbi Baruch (everyone called him 'Rabbi Barokh' because Rabbis enjoyed the privilege, as did great lords, of being referred to by their title and first name), with his straight nose, delicate lips, and imperious black beard, did not need to take any special pains to appear commanding and austere. He had made himself a soldier in the Sabbath's vanguard, vigilantly announcing its arrival. As if he had been given this mission by some divine decree providing advance justification for despotic severity, he never failed, no matter what the weather or season, to make his inspection late on Friday afternoons. A good hour before the official beginning of the Sabbath, he arrived, looking severe, without a word, without a smile, on 'the boulevard,' the neighborhood's commercial artery. He proceeded with long, energetic steps, his ample black rabbinical robe slapping his heels. Using his cane, which he brandished like a cutlass, he occasionally struck resounding blows on the wooden doorframes to tell the merchants it was time to close their shops. Everyone hastened to obey: the pastry shop owner put up his trays (almost empty at this time of day) and the grocer dealt, grumbling, with his last customers. As for the merchants who walked about selling to children the indispensable Sabbath treats (black, anise flavored candy; pumpkin, watermelon, and sunflower seeds; roasted chickpeas), they waited until the very last minute to pack up their wares. But Rabbi Barokh did not leave until he had made a clean sweep and there was not a single shop still open. The neighborhood was then ready to properly welcome Queen Sabbath, and the rabbi, his soul temporarily at peace, could return home, before going to lead the evening service in the synagogue that bore his name.

Rabbi Joseph ('Rabbi Yossef') was, in outward appearance, the exact opposite of Rabbi Baruch: one had a pale, severe face, the other an engaging, ruddy face. If one of them represented the Law in its austere rigor, the other seemed to be the incarnation of goodwill, flexibility, and gentleness. To the Sabbath celebrations, he made a contribution I found fascinating: his *drach*, that is, his sermon. We literally crowded – a throng composed of all the generations – into the 'new synagogue,' which never had enough room when he was speaking. His low and slightly raspy voice quickly made the overheated audience fall silent. Everyone strained to hear him. Then began a homily of a very special kind. It started with a simple verse from the Sefer Torah, chosen from the selection that had been read that very morning. To interpret its meaning, the learned orator relied first on Rashi. Then he developed, as if they were obvious, points I did not understand at all, playing with the letters of certain words, either transforming them into numbers, which he compared with other numbers obtained in the same way, or making them the first letter of new words that turned out to be particularly rich in meaning. Afterward, he descended from the heights of speculation and became more accessible. And also more familiar, and even funny at times. He told a great many anecdotes and parables. Thanks to him, I learned all sorts of things my mother had never thought of telling me (did she even know them?): for example, that for the Sabbath, Jews are endowed with a second soul, that on that day the forces of evil are deprived of their power, and even the flames in Hell cease to burn; or that the Angel of Death cannot carry anyone off who is studying the Torah. But as the end of the sermon approached, his voice grew serious again. Quotations from the Bible and the Talmud appeared with increasing frequency and, as soon as they were recognized, were repeated in chorus by most of those present, who were delighted to have a chance to respond to the master. And the sermon ended, the audience hushed and spellbound, with some splendid evocation of the messianic age. I left the synagogue stunned, intoxicated with new wisdom, and happy.

In spite of the pleasure – which was sometimes intense – I took in these reminiscences, they remained intermittent. Things, and especially words, came to me in a jerky, inconsistent manner. I had not succeeded in making writing a regular activity.

I was not much concerned by this apparent disorder, for I was certain I was on the right path: I now felt myself bound to my project as much by necessity as by natural inclination.

Nevertheless, I had to endure the gently ironic incredulity of my friends, particularly those at the École Normale, when I mentioned the progress of my work – I did this less and less often – without daring to show them, and for good reason, anything I had actually written. It seemed to them frivolous, and they didn't hesitate to tell me so: it was one thing to spice up my conversation with a few details drawn from my exotic past, carefully selected to attract or amuse an audience whose taste for this sort of thing had long been known to me; it was another to make these details, at my age and in a period as difficult as the one we were living through, virtually my only concern!

I let them talk. To reply, to try to justify this apparent violation of the values of openness and universalism that governed us would have been to suggest that I was claiming some sort of privilege because I was different, that I was putting in question at least some aspects of our years of common daily life. This was a misunderstanding to which I had no desire to expose myself; for in truth, I regarded these years as just as important as those of my childhood from which I was trying to free myself. On the contrary, I was proud, *in petto*, of having been able to focus my idle faculties on a single object: I thought of the Roman matrons who took pride in having had only one husband, or of the ascetics who, finding their tiny cells still too large, went to live on top of a column. At that time I took shelter, with an eclecticism I liked to see as provocative, behind two solid – and in my view, prophetic – precepts. One (which I obviously did not interpret as calling for narcissistic complacency but rather as encouraging persistence) was addressed to me by Plotinus: he enjoined me 'never to cease sculpting my own statue.' The other, picked up somewhere (probably secondhand, since at that time Cocteau was definitely not one of 'my' authors), I had written with great care on the file folder in which I kept the fragments I'd more or less composed: 'Whatever people reproach in you, cultivate it, it is your very self.'

I even drew a kind of moral satisfaction from what seemed to me, on certain days, to be a courageous act. I had been particularly moved, ever since my first conversations with my mother, by the figure of the solitary, persecuted hero who has had the misfortune to be ahead of his time. In this case, I was sure that I was blazing a new trail and I sometimes still think nostalgically that, had I been more persevering, I might have been able to serve as a precursor for all the young Sephardic authors – most of them children of French colonials who had returned to France, which I was not – who were also to discover, in the 1970s, their distinctiveness and to try to define it, in one way or another.

And then there were moments of excitement in which serious questions brutally surged up, like a challenge to the smooth humming of my memory-exploring machine. I could not avoid making an attempt to find answers to these questions. I remember, for example, laboring for a long time over what I had called 'the dark spots' or 'the shadowy areas.'

Like many apprentice writers, I had taken to heart, while reading great authors, the adage according to which good feelings and good literature don't go together. Too many of the fragments of my future epic seemed to me, with the exception of a few small details, to be bathed in a rosy light. True, we were not the Atrides, nor any of those other accursed family lines whose misfortunes are transformed, in the expert hands of poets, into tragedies for the ages. In all the materials I had collected, there was nothing –

save my proudly proclaimed allegiance to my dear Ben Abouya – that was violent, subversive, iconoclastic, or heretical. It seemed to me that I had to correct this defect as soon as possible. It was crazy, at a time when Sade, Bataille, and Genet were becoming obligatory models for every minor scribbler, to try to put on the market a book in which there were no seducers, madmen, thieves, or murderers. Lacking the sanguinary torrents that flowed elsewhere, I had to set out in search of this indispensable material: a few drops of blood or sperm, a few pinches of depravity, in short, a few things that would enrich the rather thin broth I was preparing for the reader.

It took me a while to find them, so fully had I interiorized the family's perspective on the world. As if the taboos that for us ruled out whole domains of life – and especially those related to sex, death, suffering, and violence in all its forms – continued to act in spite of time and distance. Nonetheless, I said to myself as I was digging through my memories, there must have been, in our family as well, the inevitable percentage of nuts, crooks, maniacs, or unfortunates that one normally finds in any community! I reviewed all the anecdotes I had collected: which ones had some shocking aspect that could serve my ends? I found nothing. Nothing that was capable of competing, so far as transgression was concerned, with the most anodyne episodes in contemporary novels. No aged mother in a dark hovel, abandoned by her family after a life of sacrifice; no son who had become a pimp, crook, or lock picker; no young woman prematurely worn out by alcohol or debauchery; no outlaw brother whose name an angry patriarch had strictly forbidden anyone to utter. Or else it would have been necessary, in order to produce something sufficiently appalling, to blacken a few insignificant details. Was I going to try to transform into sulfurous stories of incest the marriages between cousins I had noted down? Or rather, inverting a murderer's usual way of proceeding, disguise as a villainous crime, whose mysterious circumstances I would have to invent, some accidental or premature death? Should I give some placid second cousin, quietly growing old in comfortable celibacy, a guilty secret he had kept hidden since his youth and which gnawed away at him like a tumor? Or should I exaggerate as much as possible a neighbor's eccentricities and peculiarities in order to make him a truly unusual figure, as extravagant as one could hope to find?

I foresaw the protests this would probably elicit. All those who thought they recognized any detail, no matter how tiny, concerning someone close to them would cry: Malice! Defamation! Calumny! They would never understand that by blurring their features, by transforming their images to the point of caricature, I sought only to establish the necessary novelistic balance between dark and light, that I was, in short, yielding to purely literary necessities. And besides, if I was reduced to that point, why shouldn't I go all the way? Why shouldn't I repeat my recent exploits in tracing my ancestors, by simply annexing cataclysms found outside the family? Still too timid, and confined within the ideology of critical realism (it's not so easy to shrug off a certain dogmatism, especially when one shares it, in all good faith, with one's closest friends), I could not bring myself to take this step.

Fortunately, I could always fall back, in order to introduce the indispensable negative touch, on the world outside the family and the community. First of all, on the countless misfortunes connected with the ups and downs of Moroccan history, which was naturally to serve as the framework for my epic: like any self-respecting history, it furnished enough bloodthirsty princes, corrupt viziers, debauched courtesans, renegades, and criminals to populate any number of Shakespearean dramas. But clearly that was true only for ancient times. For the more recent period,

I would have to stress instead the confused mixture of fears, dreads, and phantasms that had been, during much of my childhood, inseparable from the utterance of the simple words *the Arabs*. For in the relatively simple universe in which I lived, *the Arabs* represented the other side, perceived as opaque, mysterious, unpredictable, and potentially laden with dangers. A naive interiorization of worn-out colonial clichés? No doubt. But the fact is that when I was seven or eight years old, I had often suffered from an unbearable nightmare, which sometimes recurred every few days. A nightmare that was so deeply anchored in my psyche that it came back again later on, several times, during the 1960s. I had written it down – at a time that I cannot, unfortunately, determine – in this way:

For some reason that now escapes me, I am crossing the medina, or rather I am coming down from the Beni-M'hamed quarter toward the new mellah. A few Arabs, all male, are silently following me. I walk along, furtively turning my head from time to time to see how many there are. The more I see, the faster I try to walk. But my feet refuse to obey me. They gradually sink into the ground, meld with it, and finally disappear altogether. The crowd of Arabs surrounds me. Some of them laugh and point at me. I'm terrified. Someone suddenly comes along who is not an Arab (a Jew, a European?). I try to run toward him. Impossible. Then I try to attract his attention by shouting. No sound emerges from my mouth, it has become as hard as wood. I wave my arms, more and more feebly. The man disappears without having seen me. I'm sweating. I have only one hope left: there might be someone in the crowd who knows my family, recognizes me. The people around me are talking more and more loudly. I attempt to cry for help. With an effort that seems to me superhuman, I succeed in uttering, but very indistinctly, something like 'Mama.' Drenched in sweat, I open my eyes.

It takes me a while to understand that my nightmare is over.

I remember that on certain evenings, for fear of having this dreadful dream again, I stubbornly refused to go to bed, or else, once in bed, I forced myself to keep my eyes open as long as possible.

This phantasm of 'the Arab attack' was not wholly gratuitous. It was fed by many stories I had heard my father tell. The one about the 1911 siege was the most striking. We had carefully preserved, in my family, the memory of those tragic hours: my father and my two grandfathers had been directly involved, since some of the mellah's defenders had assembled on the terrace of the family house.

But there was also the memory of more recent incidents, which I had myself witnessed, when I was five or six years old. Like the one that occurred one festival morning (Yom Kippur or Rosh Hashanah) at the time when people were coming out of the synagogues: groups of howling young Arabs moving through the neighborhood's streets, the cold, flinty sound of stones hitting the doors of houses, the echoes of a few gunshots coming from the direction of the new cemetery, the long wait, behind closed shutters, until night fell, and the next day, the unspoken fear that the attackers would return, which was always a possibility.

Thus it was difficult not to include, among the direct causes of my childish fears, the fearsome Aissaouas, who long played the role of bogeymen. The mere mention of the name of this brotherhood, whose sanctuary was in Meknès, right near the old mellah, made me shiver. They were supposed to have committed such horrors! It was said that you could recognize them by the long braid they wore on top of their heads (which inevitably reminded me of the cruel Chinese torturers who appeared in films like *Fu Manchu*). I never had an opportunity to check this, except much later, and then only in photographs. For me, they always remained faceless. I could only imagine, on the basis of furtive allusions, the wild abandon of their annual festivals, full of howling like that of wild animals, frenetic dances, and the ferocity that led those taking part in them to disembowel live animals with their own hands and then devour them (rams, lambs, goats, kids), and to also eat snakes, scorpions, even shards of broken glass. I was surprised to discover later that all this – which I was on the point of attributing to exaggeration, or even fabrication – closely resembled the dionysiac rituals Euripides describes in the *Bacchae.*

Maintained by these various causes, the vague unease that dwelt in me had not weighed on my dreams alone; it had also other, more comical effects. It had, for instance, disproportionately increased my respect for the French police, who were very popular in a neighborhood that thought it could count on their help and protection. However, being uncomfortably quartered in a tiny shack near the market, there were never more than two or three of them, accompanied by as many Moroccan assistants, the *mokhazni*. But their handsome navy blue uniforms, their buttons shining in the sun, their broad, visored caps, and the enormous pistol which, in its leather holster, always hung from their belts, had become for me the very image of security.

This led me to want a firearm for myself. By the time I was ten, this desire had become intense, almost obsessive. *Browning, Colt, automatic,* and *revolver* had become part of my everyday vocabulary. I took an interest in brands, calibers, and even the weight and shape of different models, as well as the price of ammunition. But while awaiting the miracle that would put me in possession of the marvelous jewel I dreamed about, and which would make me invulnerable, I had to be satisfied with vulgar, flimsy popguns that came on the scene only as Purim approached and disappeared shortly afterward, leaving me disarmed for the rest of the year.

Could I decently, after having made this inventory, append to the list of my 'dark spots' a few incidents in family life that I had not yet been able to fit into my various outlines? This would undeniably be a stretch, given the great distance separating the tragedies I would have liked to write about and the minor inconveniences I was going to have to relate. In the end, I nevertheless resolved to adopt this strategy, telling myself that it was, like all the rest, merely provisional, and that there would always be an opportunity to make adjustments in the final version. That is how I came to describe what I called 'the torments of the new suit.'

Several weeks before Passover, my mother had decided it was time to 'think about the children's festival clothes.' This immediately became an emergency and had to be dealt with as such. But it was dealt with in two ways. For my sisters, 'the couturiere was called in' (that was the traditional way of putting it), accompanied by a couple of young apprentices. An appointment had to be made long in advance, because this was the busiest time of the year for her. She stayed at our house for several days, transforming our patio into a workshop full of laughter and gaiety, into which I slipped on the slightest excuse. I was capable of remaining motionless and silent for a long time, watching the boss cutting up the bolts of cloth with her scissors, and her workers assembling the pieces that were to become my sisters' festival garments. Sometimes I was allowed to gather up the scraps, and this made me inexplicably happy. But especially, crawling about on all fours among the chairs, I loved to pick up, using a big magnet, the thimbles and pins that had fallen all over the floor. After being tried on and refitted many times, the dresses were ready.

They would be hung from a big wooden rod in my parents' armoire and come out again only when they were ceremoniously donned on the first morning of the festival.

As for myself, things proceeded in an entirely different way. The making of a new suit was a trial to which I resigned myself less and less willingly. It was a process with several stages: the choice and purchase of a fabric in a shop, the choice of a tailor, the choice of a style, the measurements, the fitting and adjustment sessions. From beginning to end, this could easily take five or six weeks. Each stage involved repeated, tiring visits: the fabric merchants' shops were all in a sort of bazaar in the middle of a densely populated, noisy, crowded neighborhood that was almost wholly unknown to me; and the tailors to whom my mother usually went had their workshops in parts of the old mellah into which I had never had occasion to go. But above all, there was the annoyance of witnessing, silent and powerless, a scene that seemed to me utterly absurd. The fabric merchant, who in general spoke only Arabic, thought he had to praise extravagantly the materials he laid out (they were almost always described as being English). My mother, not attempting to conceal her skepticism, took the sample and subjected it to various kinds of manipulation: she began by feeling it, next she weighed it, and then, taking it out of the shop, which was always too dark, she examined it in the sunlight for a long time, trying to find and decipher the manufacturer's mark woven into the cloth. When she finally felt confident that the fabric was of good quality, she turned to me to ask whether I liked the color. I always replied that I did, because I was so eager to get it over with. Then there remained the part I found, in my nascent pride, the most disagreeable: the bargaining. I didn't like seeing my mother involved in these charades: although they were common enough, they seemed to me somehow humiliating. Therefore I averted my eyes, furious. I even ended up, in my exasperation, by inventing a sort of game. A game played only in my head: I went out of the shop for a moment, leaving my mother the vile merchant's prisoner, and immediately came back in, loaded down – like the drummer boy in the song – with gold and jewels, by means of which I succeeded in rescuing her. This did not shorten the negotiations by one second, but the imaginary vengeance prevented me from suffering too much.

I would have so much preferred a simpler, less trying solution: quickly purchasing a ready-made suit like the ones I saw, worn by blond mannequins, in the display windows of the city's only large department store (Lanoma, which was later replaced by the Galeries Lafayette), in front of which I always lingered when returning from the movies on Saturday. But the family finances, at that point, did not allow such dreams to be realized. Thus, to my great despair, for a long time still (right up to my departure for Paris), I had to make do with the sober productions of our old local tailors, which were more affordable than the dazzling ready-made clothes imported from France I could hardly wait to put on.

THE TURNING POINT

The best writer is always
the one who secretly criticizes
what he writes.
– Louis-Sébastian Mercier,
Dictionnaire d'un polygraphe

Your memory, like dark fables,
Beats on the reader as a drum.
– Charles Baudelaire,
'Les Fleurs du mal'

However, one day the lovely mechanism began to freeze up, and the epic mirage began to dissipate. I encountered those moments when, in a lightning flash, some of the masks that ordinarily protect us fall. Our gaze suddenly becomes more acute, more penetrating. Capable, indeed, of grasping the contours of a reality that seems quite new, unrelated to the reality that up to that point has been our daily companion. In this case, the message was simple and final: Dead end! No outlet! Wrong way! What I was putting together was one of those all too common compositions born to end up in the literary – and domestic – form of purgatory known as the desk drawer.

I had in fact been caught up in a process which, well launched and now well worn, had no reason to end. Carried along by my natural inclination to save, to store up, I saw nothing that might someday force me to stop amassing starts, drafts, outlines, diagrams, sketches, and fragments.

The 'objective documentation,' to which the researcher's reflex had led me to devote to my initial inquiries, had piled up. Moving from articles to bibliographies and from bibliographies to more or less serious works, I had been drawn in the most diverse directions: Moroccan Judaism turned out to be a more complex, and especially a less unexplored, subject than I had at first naively believed. Everyone had made some little – or big – contribution to it: some authors wrote monographs analyzing the different types of mellahs, others dealt with linguistic, demographic, or onomastic questions, and still others offered erudite reflections on marriage ceremonies or on the conduct of pilgrimages. And I watched with increasing concern as my 'scholarly' notes (the photocopying mania had not yet arrived) piled up on the corner of my desk: it all seemed so distant, so foreign, that I had the sensation, at times, of being in Flaubert's predicament when he was getting ready to write *Salammbô!*

My 'subjective documentation' was in even worse shape. While family sources had, after a few months, exhausted their reserves and no longer had anything to offer other than minimal variations on themes already well known to me, this was not true of my own memory. I had used all sorts of techniques in exploring it. The lexical technique had proven the most productive. Armed with a tiny pocket dictionary, every day I examined, one after another, the words on a page, and I noted down, as they occurred to me, the memories that each of them evoked. It sometimes took a single line to do this, sometimes half a page, almost always in a telegraphic style; on rare occasions, I wrote a real sentence or two. My lexicon quickly grew larger. On some days you could actually see it growing. The 'file cards' (in fact, these were scraps of paper in all sizes and shapes) were piling up. I avoided classifying them. I thought it would be important, when the moment to begin writing arrived, to be able to reconstruct the precise order in which my memories had appeared: who knew what reflections, what conclusions (for instance, concerning my memory's oscillations or the strange logic of my mental associations) I would be able to draw from this? The problem was that it made consulting the lexicon difficult: when I wanted to find, for example, the file card on 'stairway' to add a couple of new references to it, I had to recall, more or less approximately, the day and the month when I had written it. But the collection of file cards became so large that I finally had to resign myself to putting them in alphabetical order.

Stimulated in this way, my memory thus continued to provide me with material for scribbling: it seemed inexhaustible.

And even when I happened – as I often did – to examine repeatedly the same fragment of the lexical field, I was always able to harvest something new from it. I seemed to be more and more like an old man who can never finish writing up his last will and testament, and who periodically feels the need to add some new codicil. Writing, instead of ridding me of my past, merely opened up whole new areas I would never have spontaneously thought about. Someone more certain of his enterprise's legitimacy would have rejoiced in this abundance, which demonstrated, at least, that my retrospective vision was relatively sharp. But I was beginning to be alarmed by it, as if it were a malignant growth. And I came almost to envy a friend who, when I told him about my memory's unfurling, tartly replied in a challenging tone: 'I have no childhood memories!'

Transforming these mounting note piles into a book seemed less and less feasible. Their roots now sank too deeply into my life, they had become part my most familiar surroundings. The living bond that connected me to them was not of the kind that can be cut without pain. I, who hate to leave anything that has kept me company, even for just an evening (to the point that I will go to great lengths to delay the departure of someone visiting my home), who have always felt a secret pang at the sight of anything that must come to an end (for I cannot help seeing in it the prefiguration of other ends) – was I going to be able to endure seeing my notes gradually dissolve, become paragraphs, pages, chapters? Besides, I knew they themselves would not go along without protest. Every time I tried to combine them, sort them, assemble them, they all – the simplest as well as the most sophisticated – resisted me in the strangest way: they literally rejected unity and cracked open like nutshells, one after another, all the forms – whether rigid or flexible – into which I was trying to fit them. As if their true vocation were to remain, obstinately, in exile and dispersion.

Anyway, they no longer satisfied me. When I compared what was in my writings with what was in my memory, I was perplexed by the disparity. As usual, reality – which I believed I had skilfully captured – had slipped away from me, and all these notes, despite their growing number, obviously did not correspond to what I wanted to say. I had tried to pour, all at once, into the narrow neck of a bottle, an enormous quantity of water; only a few drops had gotten in.

I also discovered, on rereading, that some of my memories lacked the consistency, the rock-hard stability I had attributed to them at the beginning of my research. They were evolving, appearing in changing forms, with erasures, corrections, revisions, second thoughts. Like dreams that settle in place only after several appearances, several attempts (as if the unconscious itself were uncertain as to which message to deliver), it seemed they still needed to shape themselves and ripen. At times I thought I saw them coagulating, but then they constituted themselves in clusters with unpredictable contours. And I saw how arbitrary and even illegitimate my attempts to put them down in writing had been: day after day, writing had produced various bits of narrative, none of which now seemed to me the right one.

I could have pretended not to know this or decided not to pay attention to it. All I had to do was to proclaim at the outset, loud and clear, that for me there was no truth other than the one that emerged at the moment of writing. Nothing would then prevent me from leaving as it was, without changing an iota, the magma of dreams, phantasms, and frustrations my memory had deposited along the way, which denatured the moments I had really experienced. I couldn't resign myself to this.

A resistance that was further amplified by a new and urgent

concern: I thought I saw appearing, in some of these pages, the telltale mark of an egoistic rhetoric. Up to that point I had been borne along by the illusion that I was merely a narrator whose task was to finally give a voice to all those whom I had pretentiously called 'my people'; I realized that in fact I myself was taking up most of the space in order to tell a few old personal secrets I had too carefully kept. I was afraid of having upstaged in this way the people I initially wanted to honor and of having substituted for the indispensable chronicle of 'us' the moaning complaint of an omnipresent 'I.' What did the epic I had in mind have to do with the scribe I discovered as I was rereading my notes? My project required the tumultuous violence of a verbal torrent, the excesses, the striking enthusiasm of a prodigal son; what I saw before my eyes was at best only the little coupons saved up by a small-time investor.

So difficult was it to make myself simultaneously (relatively speaking) the Virgil and the Aeneas, or the Homer and the Odysseus, of my familial Judaic Moroccan epic!

But that was not all. While I had remained feverishly engaged in groping around in the tiniest corners of the past (with a care at least the equal of that my father had taught me when, the day before Passover, we tracked down together, in every part of the house, the last dropped bread crumbs), life had gone on. And gradually, it had made my project seem less urgent, and even less necessary. After having long been in the category – more widespread than people think, and moreover perfectly honorable, in my view – of always-future books, the great saga of the Benabouyades had slipped into that of unlikely books and perhaps into that of impossible books.

The community whose past I had wanted to rehabilitate was being purely and simply driven out of history. Twenty centuries (at least) of uninterrupted Jewish life on Moroccan soil was coming to an end in a few years of irresistible disaster. The fallout from decolonization and from the Israeli-Arab conflict had completely altered the situation whose memory lived in me. From now on, the Jews of Meknès would no longer be confined within the limits that had been those of my childhood: they had left them far behind and gone by the thousands to Paris, Haifa, or Montreal. Since I knew that the experience I was trying to describe would be at best a pale reflection of the one people had gone through, and since in addition it was clear that nothing like it would be lived by anyone else, why should I go to so much trouble? My discussion would only end up disappearing into the void. I had noted one day, with malevolent pleasure, Franz Werfel's judicious prediction, reported by Max Brod in his biography of Kafka: 'No one will understand Kafka outside Tetschen-Bodenbach.' And it was with this image – that of a poor wretch hopelessly locked up in provincialism – that I thought I had to identify myself, since I was sure that nothing I had written up to that point would find the slightest response beyond Bab el Mansour or Bab el Berrima (which marked, as the oldest guidebooks to Meknès indicated, the boundary between the mella and the medina).

As for my goals of social revenge, which I had in part interiorized because I believed they were those of my parents, I was obliged to acknowledge their narrowing: they no longer had much efficacy as incitements to writing, and their role was now limited to keeping other projects from getting under way. So the tacit contract I believed I had signed with my people, the multiple indebtedness to each and all with which I felt encumbered – all that, which had long since begun to collapse subterraneously, was finally able to dissolve.

* * *

Without any possible doubt: the valiant paladin fighting on behalf of the family and the Judeo-Moroccan cause had become unrecognizable: he had, like his favorite ancestor, become *aher* (other). Over the years, life at the École Normale in Paris had gradually altered his relationship to the world and to himself. He was now caught up in a closely woven web of loves and friendships that chance encounters, immediately declared affinities, and enduring shared pleasures had allowed him to construct. In it he had found, without much difficulty, the feeling – indispensable for his peace of mind – of belonging to a family: new rites, new festivals, new models of behavior had slowly become dominant. And even new ancestors, who were henceforth named Saint Augustine or Montaigne, Diderot or Rousseau, Flaubert or Roussel. His difference, whether real or supposed, no longer much bothered him. He felt he had arrived at the culmination of a long ascent: an ascent toward a self seen as totally free, or almost -- free at least to make choices about his future – and no longer determined by some burdensome geographical or religious necessity. Grandiose urges, boundless desires, vague and magnanimous dreams – he was prepared to attach himself to all the intersecting currents swirling around him, to plunge into the politico-cultural turmoil of his new homeland, the Latin Quarter of the 1960s. In other words, he felt called upon to undertake other tasks that were still more pressing . . . even his university work had been affected by this change in direction. He had, after many doubts and not without regret, bidden a provisional farewell to literary studies in order to take up history. Gorged on antiquity, his head stuffed with Greek and Latin lore, he had chosen to study Roman Africa. And, henceforth devoting most of his time to this research, it seemed to him that he had paid off a debt owed ancestors more remote than those with whom he had been previously concerned. His imaginary family line, the catchall genealogy he had cobbled together through successive appropriations, did not send him back to the Jews alone. It also led him a little further, toward the most ancient inhabitants of North Africa, the Berbers whom Greek and Roman historians had more or less ignored or maligned. To win his pardon for having once taken his leave of them – without any hope of returning – in order to keep that rupture from looking to him like an evasion, he had to claim them, even rehabilitate them if he could. Afterward, and only afterward, could he leave them in peace without regret.

Meager and laughable, that is how my unfortunate Meknèssian getup now struck me. And how narrow, compared with the literatures that were then being discovered and so much admired! Apparently irreversible political upheavals in whole continents, in Latin America, in Black Africa, had just made their entrance on the cultural stage, with their (vast) spaces, (flourishing) vitality, (lyrical) energy, or (epic) spirit that carried them forward. And I – at the same time, was I going to rattle, under the beds of young mothers, ancient, rusty sabers, reopen old wounds everyone, including me, had half forgotten? From then on I had to rein in my impulses, do everything I could to avoid what had earlier seemed unavoidable. After all, why should I hesitate to free myself from a slavery into which only my own will had cast me?

Nevertheless, to help me take the necessary step and altogether convince me, certain chance events were necessary: two episodes, connected with a sudden irruption of the past, provided me with an opportunity to truly rediscover, at least partially, some of the people and voices of my childhood.

The first episode. This took place on a grassy lawn in Natanya, near the sea, on a luminous Saturday morning in spring: a few dozen ex-residents of Meknès, who had emigrated some time ago and had taken up residence in the principal cities of Israel, had agreed to meet there for their annual get-together, a ritual they had been observing with persistent assiduity for a long time. One of my cousins, who was also becoming fascinated by our common history (to which he was to make, a few years later, many important contributions), was taking part in this. Knowing that I was passing through, he had invited me. I had accepted, not without a certain apprehension.

I had not seen these people, most of them, since the beginning of the 1950s, some of them not since the summer of 1948 when the first great emigrations took place. They were almost all there: faces, looks, gestures, tones of voice, all suddenly familiar again. And immediately, along with them, reappeared a few episodes of common activity, a few shared moments.

One of these was waking up at dawn, on certain days, in order to have time to attend, before school or lycée, the earliest morning service: the faithful, few in number in the little synagogue at that hour, were pressed for time, as we were; prayers were said at such a rapid pace – the Hebrew words seeming to slip, disembodied and reduced to an imperceptible whisper, between the lips of the person reciting them – that I quickly lost my place; then I had to hurriedly flip through my prayerbook at the risk of tearing the pages in my haste, apprehensively trying to catch up with the leaders of the pack.

And, on the first fine days of spring, the first games of marbles under the false pepper trees in the schoolyard while our teachers were talking among themselves, and the director, majestic and alone, carelessly slicking down his mustache with his forefinger, walked back and forth in front of his open office, waiting to imperiously notify us all by stridently blowing his police whistle (which was the revered and yet simultaneously dreaded instrument of his directorial omnipotence) that recess was over.

And the games and singing sessions, on Wednesday evenings or Sunday mornings, in a sort of lean-to garage, small and dimly lit, which served as a clubhouse for the Cub Scout pack we all belonged to. Divided into 'sixes,' each with its own leader, we learned about Mowgli, Akela, Bagheera, and all the animals in *The Jungle Book*, as well as about Baden-Powell and the joys of scouting. All we thought about was hikes, totems, pennants, and singing under the stars around the campfire. And I had – gladly – given up my music lessons because they coincided with the pack's meeting times.

And, on the last afternoon before the end of Passover – when we were already beginning to consider that we had met the strict dietary requirements scrupulously observed during the preceding seven days – racing through the open fields that surrounded the neighborhood: we went to gather nearly ripe kernels of wheat and wildflowers, which we brought home by the handful in order to decorate the Mimouna table.

And, finally, the moments of tensely hurrying along, keeping close together, when we had to run the daily gauntlet through the medina: at every street corner, three or four ragged Arab kids might suddenly appear, whose main occupation seemed to be lying in wait in order pelt us, as hard as they could and hitting us in the face if possible, with volleys of stones collected for that purpose.

In the middle of the little group that had spontaneously formed around the unexpected visitor that I was, while conversation proceeded in a chaotic mixture of Hebrew, Judeo-Arabic, and French, I felt something dormant coming back to life: echoes from the past drew nearer, inflections became intimate, the tone turned confidential. And for the first time, although I was not in any way expecting it, I sensed that my perspective on my life was wavering.

What I had to tell, to summarize before these interlocutors who had risen up from the old days and who were eager for news was no longer, as I had assumed on a hundred occasions since my arrival in Paris, the sweet delights of an exotic childhood; it was, on the contrary, the routine that had become my adult life: classical studies, examinations, academic competitions, working in the university. But whereas I regarded this as a major break with our common past, they considered it a natural, expected, even foreseeable continuation of this same past. For – and it took me a while to see this behind their half-smiles and unspoken assumptions – the only conceivable rupture was clearly the one they themselves had made, by going to Israel. As for myself, in their view I had only exchanged one 'exile' for another . . .

The second episode took place in the fall of the same year. One of my childhood friends who had become a filmmaker had decided to make a long documentary on the small minority of Jews remaining in Morocco. He had gone to shoot it on location and had accorded particular importance to Meknès, lingering with feeling on the places where we had, both of us, grown up. Naturally, I rushed off to see the film, which was very successful. I came out with a mixed impression.

Joy in seeing come really to life on the screen all the images that had remained, for so many years, abstract and rigid, mere memory traces slumbering in some recess of the cerebral cortex.

Images of people. The same Arab merchant, only a little more wrinkled and slightly portly, was still padding about the neighborhood streets, singing, in the same dry voice, the same little song in praise of his merchandise, an unusual treat which, so far as I know, he alone sold: a broad, thin spiral of nougat, twisted like ivy around a tree trunk, which, when bitten off in small pieces, at first crackled under the teeth and then softened into a syrupy mass. But since the little Jewish kids had almost all left, what customers did he have now?

Images of the rows of façades that I recognized, for the most part, at first glance: the leafy garden of the 'Villa Elghrably,' the three steps leading up to the house of my Toledano cousins, the Elkrief's veranda . . .

Images of the rectilinear streets along which my mother had dragged me when she took me to Talmud Torah but which I had also – a proper reward for my efforts – passed down in triumph a few years later, on the day of my bar mitzvah (which we called, by a curious process of imitation, 'first communion'): perched on a dark red velvet armchair in a brand-new navy blue twill suit, white shirt, and bow tie, preceded by two musicians and followed by the noisy cortege of my friends, cousins, and classmates, as I went along I handed out treats and cigarettes (customarily allowed on that day, as if attaining religious adulthood also gave you the right to smoke).

Images of a few prominent buildings. The great café-restaurant at the sign of Jacob's Well, with its double façade on a corner at the very heart of the neighborhood, where so many festivals had been celebrated, and above all, the very first marriage ceremony I attended (I had been encouraged, by my teacher himself, to skip school). The other restaurant, more modest, with its open-air terrace, down below 'the boulevard,' where I had long dreamed of going to taste at least once the Saturday evening brochettes, which smelled so good on the big charcoal oven where they were grilled (but my mother, for hygienic reasons, would not allow this, and it was some time before I dared disobey her on this point).

And the school where I had been a pupil for five years: my career there being completed on the day – which had remained memorable for me – on which, under a blazing sun, on the occasion of the solemn awarding of prizes (this was the first one since the end of the war, and it coincided exactly with my eleventh birthday), I had to play the leading role, that of the husband, in *La Farce de la femme muette,* before receiving from the hands of the 'authorities' – the pasha and the general having been brought together, for the event, with the president of the community and the chief rabbi – the heavy, bound volume with gilt pages (*Peau de pêche*) that gave concrete form, finally and very agreeably, to the previously highly abstract notion of a 'prize for excellence.'

And also the joy of seeing the camera linger on certain details of what had been our house: the double ironwork door, painted black, the long entry hall leading to the kitchen, the large central room and its multicolored mosaics, the star-shaped basin with its water fountain in the middle of the garden.

But as for the rest of the film, made up chiefly of live interviews and inside scenes, I could not conceal my dismay on seeing what the camera had implacably succeeded in capturing and transmitting to me. One moment in particular struck me. It was the evening of Mimouna (which marks the end of Passover) in the home of an old family in Fez. The big table was covered with all the foods required by tradition: a large cup overflowing with immaculate flour, in which unshelled green beans were stuck, along with a few pieces of gold and silver; all around, a big pitcher of fresh milk and another of whey; then came the countless kinds of cakes and, in addition to the customary almond confections, the two specialities of the day: a very white nougat, soft in consistency and still somewhat liquid, and dark brown preserves made from raisins and nuts. Around the table, a few old men with creaky voices, their mouths full of conventional expressions that were supposed to be reassuring and reassured but rang false, pitifully false. Rigid postures that sought – without much conviction – to imitate the joy of olden times. A determination to go on acting as if...

In spite of myself, I could not avoid making the diagnosis: clearly, there was nothing much to celebrate in this world, which had essentially outlived itself.

And I was suddenly gripped by uneasiness. Who knows? Maybe this was already true of my childhood as well? Maybe I was in the process of creating, by means of reconstructed memories, tendentious testimonies, and unverifiable legends, a purely mythical universe? Everything I had been able to collect for my epic was therefore from the outset subject to legitimate suspicion. The setting? I was going to describe atmospheres drawn from oriental tales in a place where, perhaps, there had been nothing more than insignificant decors: naked façades hastily daubed with whitewash a few days before the festivals, shaky balconies of rusty ironwork, tiny gardens with neglected vegetation, ochre-colored stone walls eaten away by the July sun. My ancestors? I was going to try to construct their figures out of whole cloth by attributing to each of them distinctive but complementary traits with a single end in view: to allow the least practiced eye to discern in them, in a sketchy form, the main lines of our future destiny. But by giving them more or less emblematic characters, I would probably have ended up only with synthetic figures, like the ancient divinities who were represented, in some works of the Renaissance, weighed down with various attributes that were occasionally very difficult to reconcile. In order to correct this defect, was I going to try, beforehand, to slip inside their skins? But they would then be just so many impostors, since I would have endowed them with a psychology more or less borrowed from my own, and they would ultimately seem to proceed from me rather than I from them. I wondered whether I was not going to resemble the black king (the story is told by Heine) who, having his portrait painted by a European artist, wanted to be 'painted as a white man.'

Henceforth, nothing seemed to me satisfactory. Not even the choice of the epic or novelistic form. Had I been right to resort to this outdated formula? It was clear that it was not suited to my abilities: my mind was much too abstract, much too attracted to systems and combinatory games, to be able to give birth to flesh and blood characters; moreover, instead of limiting myself to showing, I inevitably yielded to my penchant for telling, for explanation and commentary.

Was I going to remain in this uncomfortable position for a long time, like the monkey who, hanging from a tree branch, tries to grab the moon in the water and persists in the attempt until one day he gets tired and lets go, disappearing into the pond?

OVER AND OVER

*If the secret history of books could be
written, and the authors's private thoughts
and meanings noted down alonsgside of
his story, how many insipid volumes would
become interesting, and dull tales excite
the reader!* – Thackeray, *Pendennis*

My project was teetering on the brink of failure.

This peculiar hybrid of exotic tale, colonial history, and family epic, which I also had to convert into a weapon of social revenge, was not to be realized anytime soon. I had nonetheless shown that I could wait for a long – a very long – time, and such patience, I had been told as a child, is indispensable for the emergence of genius. But what should I do, faced by this new discovery? What I had begun as a promising project, rich in satisfying and comforting possibilities, had been transformed into a chore that could never be completed.

I had fallen into the first trap life had set for me. Or rather, I had not even waited for life to set this trap for me. Heedlessly I had sought it out and had succeeded only in getting lost in the labyrinth that I myself had meticulously built. Therefore it was better to back off and forget the whole thing.

Besides, I told myself, repeating one of my childhood questions, is a book the normal outcome of every writing project? While I had, at certain moments, attempted to persuade myself that this was true, I had not been wholly successful, and I had no regrets about that. The simple expression 'write a book,' as banal as it was, had very early on begun to seem strange to me. In all logic, I argued with a twelve-year-old's earnestness, it ought to be used only in the past tense, after the object (the book) produced by the action implied by the verb (to write) has been brought into existence; therefore it is impossible to simply say: 'I am writing a book.' That would assume that the book exists prior to the act of writing, whereas it is only one of the possible results – desired, hoped for, but not in any way guaranteed – of that very act. Hence I was ready to give up, without too many regrets, while at the same time thinking – in the greatest secrecy, naturally, for one doesn't talk about such things – about someday realizing a different goal: making the unfinished and unfinishable book not an unfortunate result of my incompetence, but rather a genuine literary genre with its own norms and rules.

Years went by. Ten years. Then twenty. Then thirty. During all that time, I was now and then obliged to recognize that my youthful project had not disappeared. Then I thought of the Berber women who are believed to be sterile but are in fact bearing within themselves a 'sleeping child' and will give birth only when it pleases the child to awaken. To be sure, in its new environment, my memory had finally learned restraint and discretion. But it had stubbornly refused to give up its rights, and, to show that it intended to exercise them one day, it sent me, in various forms (recurrent dreams connected with the streets of Meknès, a disproportionate emotional response to certain odors, tastes, or sounds), absolutely unambiguous messages. As for my writing, which during all that time had gone nowhere, except (with a few minor exceptions) from one dead end to another, it had succeeded in managing, through this very movement, to survive. It survived, however, only in a form that was very furtive. Evanescent. In bits. Almost impalpable. And which soon concentrated on a concern that became an obsession: giving at least my initial lines – whose inaugural vocation I had superstitiously never dared question and which had therefore become virtually the incarnation of my whole project – the follow-up they were still, subterraneously, awaiting.

Up until the day on which a new attempt, at first unsuccessful like all the earlier ones, nevertheless set in motion a mechanism that produced unanticipated results. Yes, I had suddenly understood (why the devil did it take me so long?) that my incipit would have a continuation only if I stopped trying to give it one. How? Well, by finally letting it remain simply an isolated fragment and presenting it as such from the outset. Then all I had to do was take this bit of flotsam as my support and let myself be carried along by it.

I had happened to discover – thanks to my preparatory readings at the time when I was searching everywhere for a Jewish model for my epic – a few fragments of Hassidic literature. I had been struck by one point, which I had duly written down in my notes: the importance accorded narratives of the words and deeds of the movement's great masters. For the Hassidim, so far as I could see, a narrative is quite different from, and far more than, a verbal reflection of a past reality. It perpetuates, through its very words, the sacred essence from which it proceeds. So that one can, on occasion, reiterate a miracle simply by recounting it. 'We cannot light the fire, we can no longer say prayers, we no longer know where,' said Rabbi Israel of Rhizhin when the moment came to reproduce a miracle accomplished by one of his predecessors, 'but we can tell the story.' And that was enough. I had long admired this magical virtue, and not without a touch of envy. In the predicament in which I found myself, couldn't I try to turn it to my very egoistic advantage? I certainly didn't have to reproduce a miracle. All I wanted to take from my Hassidic reference was the 'we can tell the story,' the conviction – oh, how reassuring it was! – that a story has the power to bring about the results of the action it relates.

Thus equipped, I could straddle my bit of flotsam and, starting out from my old incipit, let my story drift along. All I had to do was find the indispensable compass that would tell me which direction to take.

It was once again in Jewish tradition that I was, by chance, to find it – or more precisely, in the writings of certain Kabalists whom I would have very much liked, through some genealogical trick, to attach to my family. Replacing the first word of Genesis with one of its anagrams (*Bereshit*, 'In the beginning,' thus becoming *Besheerit*, 'with the remains'), they had dared to make an assertion whose audacity astounded me: the whole of creation – yes, the majestic edifice of creation, with heaven and earth, and the two lamps placed in the firmament to light the earth, and the waters teeming with swarms of living beings – is made only from debris, fragments, residues.

Thanks to their intuition – duly reduced to the dimensions of my little problem of literary creation – I could finally identify the form miraculously accorded my situation and my capacities. Neither a heroic epic, nor a flamboyant saga, nor a great classical novel. Rather, an attempt to assemble, within a narrative that had to be begun over and over – for I am convinced that one always writes the same book – the scattered remains of a work destined to remain unfinished.

In the *Stages* series

Volume 1
*The Rushdie Letters: Freedom to Speak,
Freedom to Write.* Edited by Steve
MacDonogh in association with Article 19

Volume 2
Mimologics. By Gérard Genette
Edited and translated by Thaïs Morgan

Volume 3
Playtexts: Ludics in Contemporary Literature
By Warren Motte

Volume 4
*New Novel, New Wave, New Politics:
Fiction and the Representation of History in
Postwar France.* By Lynn A. Higgins

Volume 5
*Art for Art's Sake and Literary Life: How
Politics and Markets Helped Shape the
Ideology and Culture of Aestheticism, 1790–
1990.* By Gene H. Bell-Villada

Volume 6
*Semiotic Investigations: Towards an
Effective Semiotics.* By Alec McHoul

Volume 7
Rue Ordener, Rue Labat. By Sarah Kofman
Translated by Ann Smock

Volume 8
Palimpsests: Literature in the Second Degree
By Gérard Genette. Translated by
Channa Newman and Claude Doubinsky

Volume 9
The Mirror of Ideas. By Michel Tournier
Translated by Jonathan F. Krell

Volume 10
Fascism's Return: Scandal, Revision, and Ideology since 1980. Edited by Richard J. Golsan

Volume 11
Jacob, Menahem, and Mimoun: A Family Epic
By Marcel Bénabou
Translated by Steven Rendall